FAITH AMID APOSTASY

FRANK B. HOLBROOK

Pacific Press Publishing Association
Boise, Idaho
Oshawa, Ontario, Canada

Edited by Bonnie Tyson-Flyn
Designed by Tim Larson
Cover art by John Steele
Typeset in 10/12 New Century Schoolbook

The author assumes full responsibility for the accuracy of all
facts and quotations cited in this book.

Unless otherwise indicated, Scripture references in this book
are from the Revised Standard Version.

Library of Congress Cataloging-in-Publication Data:

Holbrook, Frank B.
    Faith amid apostasy : Jeremiah / Frank B. Holbrook.
      p.   cm.
    Includes bibliographical references.
    ISBN 0-8163-1186-2
    1. Bible. O.T. Jeremiah—Criticism, interpretation, etc.
  2. Bible. O.T. Lamentations—Criticism, interpretation, etc.
I. Title. II. Title: Jeremiah.
BS1525.2.H62   1994
224'.206—dc20   93-31717
                                              CIP

94 95 96 97 98 ● 5 4 3 2 1

Contents

Preface

Believers readily identify with Jeremiah's experiences. He is the Peter of the Old Testament—the most colorful of the Old Testament prophets. We have more information about him than we do for any other of the ancient seers. We also have more insights into his own spiritual wrestlings, since he freely records his conversations with God—his fears, his questions, his doubts and arguments.

A lifetime prophet, Jeremiah ministered to Judah during that nation's last forty years of sovereignty before the Babylonian captivity. The Lord did not remove the mountains of difficulty that faced the young man when he accepted prophetic office as God's mouthpiece. He only promised to make Jeremiah like an iron pillar and a bronze wall. The sturdy prophet never wavered publicly in his proclamation of God's word, although he endured verbal and physical abuse for his faithfulness.

Jeremiah's appeals for Judah to return to the obedience of the covenant bond fell on deaf ears. His God-prompted calls to submit to the yoke of Babylonian domination brought cries of derision and plots on his life. The princes regarded him as a traitor. At the height of the national crisis—the siege with its attendant horrors of famine and disease decimating the population—he was there encouraging the people to listen to God. And when the "lights" were going out, he still stood—a lone but important figure—pointing to God's announced plan for the peoples' future beyond the captivity!

Six hundred years later, when Jesus queried the disciples about the people's evaluation of Him, they responded with the observation that some thought (among a few other names) that Jesus might be the prophet "Jeremiah" (see Matthew 16:13, 14). Could the sleeping prophet have heard, I am sure he would have felt simultaneously honored and humbled. He would have marveled that some characteristic of his prophetic career had been reflected through the ministry of his Lord to another generation of the people!

Chapter 1

Time's Hinges

Just as large doors swing on small hinges, so great movements in human history appear now and again to pivot on insignificant events. The last quarter of the seventh century B.C. was one of those crucial periods in the Near East when the door of time opened onto a new age!

With the death of Ashurbanipal in 626 B.C. (hinge 2), the empire of Assyria reached its high-water mark. In that same year, Nabopolassar, the Chaldean, rebelled against his Assyrian overlords and proclaimed himself king of Babylon (hinge 3).[1] Twenty-one years later, his son, Nebuchadnezzar—the most famous of the Chaldean dynasty—would succeed to his throne. A few years earlier, Psamtik I of Egypt had forced the Assyrian garrison to withdraw from his kingdom (hinge 1). The crosswinds of political change had begun to swirl over the lands of the Fertile Crescent.[2]

Significantly, in 626 B.C., young Jeremiah had responded to God's call to prophetic office and joined the reform-minded Josiah, king of Judah, in a desperate attempt to save the nation from the coming storm.

As an empire (c. 900-612 B.C.) Assyria was the most warlike nation of antiquity. The national god, Ashur, was a god of war; and the people regarded military action as an act of worship. The empire exercised control over all the Fertile Crescent and neighboring areas—from the Persian Gulf to Egypt—including portions of what we know today as modern Turkey.

But now, in 626 B.C., the empire—seemingly so mighty—was dying. Its ruthless regime was about to reap its bitter rewards. The homelands began to be overrun by the Medes and Babylonians (the city of Asshur fell in 614 B.C.; Nineveh, in 612 B.C.). The Assyrians retreated to Haran in northern Mesopotamia. But by 609 B.C., their forces evicted from this last stronghold, the Assyrians ceased to be mentioned in the annals of history.

Political power struggle

The political vacuum created by the collapse of Assyria sucked down the winds of war upon the Near East. A power struggle ensued between Egypt on the Nile and the rising power of Babylon on the Euphrates, lasting for nearly a decade.

According to the Babylonian Chronicle—an incomplete series of clay tablets that provide us insight on major events in the neo-Babylonian kingdom—Egyptian forces under Pharaoh Neco, the king of Egypt, marched to the aid of the Assyrians as they were making their last stand against the Babylonians. Neco had no pity for the expiring Assyrians but hoped to extend Egyptian hegemony over Syria and Palestine by sustaining the weakened state as a buffer between an Egyptian sphere of influence and that of the rising Chaldean dynasty in Mesopotamia (see 2 Kings 23:29, RSV, NKJV).

Josiah, the last God-fearing king of Judah, was keenly aware of the death struggle between Assyria and Babylon—and Egypt's ploy to bring Syria and Palestine (including Judah) under its control. Josiah either favored the distant Babylonians over the nearby Egyptians (influenced possibly by the friendliness of the former toward his ancestor, Hezekiah, [see 2 Kings 20:12]), or he may have thought to recover by his own military prowess these same territories, which had once been a part of Solomon's realm. Without consulting God, Josiah determined to prevent the fulfillment of the Egyptian plan. Unfortunately, the decision cost him his life and Judah's national independence.

In 608 B.C. the Egyptian army crossed the Brook of Egypt, fully determined to do battle with the Babylonians in the vicinity of Carchemish by the Euphrates—a border town between Babylonia and Syria (see 2 Chronicles 35:20). Marching northward along the Way of the Sea with the Mediterranean Sea on its left, the column swung northeast upon entering the Plain of Sharon to penetrate one of three passes through the Carmel Range, exiting into the Plain of Jezreel (Esdraelon). Emerging from the pass, the Egyptian commander was surprised to find an army of Jewish soldiers near the town of Megiddo on battle alert, awaiting his arrival!

Immediately Neco dispatched a messenger to the Jews: "What have we to do with each other, king of Judah? I am not coming against you this day, but against the house with which I am at war; and God has commanded me to make haste. Cease opposing God, who is with me, lest he destroy you" (2 Chronicles 35:21).

Josiah refused. Disguising himself as one of the chariot soldiers, he committed his forces—foot and chariot—to the battle. Fighting with a detachment of chariots placed Josiah in the thick of the combat and within range of the enemy's archers. Egyptian arrows soon pierced his armor and mortally wounded the king. "Take me away, for I am badly wounded," he cried to his charioteer (verse 23).

The forces of Neco soon smashed the leaderless Judeans and left the bloody field to engage the Babylonians at Carchemish on the Euphrates. Successful, the Egyptians retired to Riblah in central Syria to establish a field headquarters from which they would spend the next three months pacifying Syria. Back in Jerusalem "the people of the land" placed twenty-three-year-old Jehoahaz, one of Josiah's sons, on the throne of Judah (see 2 Kings 23:30, 31); evidently, Josiah had not determined his successor. Jehoahaz was not Josiah's oldest son, but he may have been chosen because he favored his father's political views.

The death of Josiah and the slaughter of his army left the kingdom under the domination of Egypt. Displeased with Judah's choice when replacing Josiah, Neco summoned Jehoahaz to Riblah, deposed the youth, and sent him bound in chains to Egypt, where he later died. Neco replaced him with an older brother, to whom he gave the throne name of Jehoiakim. Judah was placed under a heavy annual tribute (one hundred talents of silver and a talent of gold), which the new king raised by taxation (see 2 Kings 23:33-35).

Peace brooded briefly over the Syrian-Palestinian lands. Then, in 605 B.C., Nebuchadnezzar decisively defeated the Egyptians at Carchemish and pursued them to Hamath in Syria, where he routed them once more. As the Babylonian army continued to tramp southward into Palestine, Nebuchadnezzar temporarily called off their pursuit of the Egyptians and brought his troops to the gates of Jerusalem. King Jehoiakim surrendered without a fight and became tributary to Babylon (see 2 Kings 24:1).

The Chaldeans spoiled the temple, taking many of its gold and silver vessels to place in the temple of their god, Marduk (see Daniel 1:1, 2; 5:2, 3). This initial invasion of Judah by Nebuchadnezzar marked the beginning stage of the Jews' Babylonian captivity. At this time Daniel and his companions and other young persons of the nobility and royalty were taken to Babylon and placed in training under Babylonian teachers (see Daniel 1:3-7).

Having secured Jehoiakim's loyalty, Nebuchadnezzar resumed his pursuit of the Egyptians. But as he approached the border of Egypt, a message reached him that his father, Nabopolassar, had died Abu 8 (August 15). By Elul 1 (September 7) Nebuchadnezzar was back in Babylon to secure his throne. Approximately three weeks elapsed between the father's death and Nebuchadnezzar's arrival back at the capital. If we allow the messenger coming from Babylon half the time, it means that the prince made the trip from the border of Egypt to Babylon in about eleven days! Josephus says that he took a short route across the Arabian desert, a feat in itself!

A third military clash between the Babylonians and the Egyptians appears to have occurred again at Carchemish in 604 B.C., resulting once more in Egypt's defeat (see Jeremiah 46:1, 2). However, according to the Babylonian Chronicle, in 601 B.C. the two superpowers again locked in a titanic struggle that left the Babylonian forces so depleted that it took Nebuchadnezzar eighteen months to recoup his losses.

But it was a Pyrrhic victory for the Egyptians. This seems to be the setting for the inspired historian's remark: "The king of Egypt did not come again out of his land, for the king of Babylon had taken all that belonged to the king of Egypt from the Brook of Egypt to the river Euphrates" (2 Kings 24:7).

Possibly Babylon's defeat this time at the hands of the Egyptians emboldened Jehoiakim to rebel against his Chaldean overlord (see 2 Kings 24:1). But that power was only temporarily delayed in its drive to rule the Near East. Roving bands, some evidently in the service of Babylon (see 2 Kings 24:2), may have been responsible for Jehoiakim's capture and imprisonment (see 2 Chronicles 36:5, 6). However, he died three months before Nebuchadnezzar and the regular troops arrived to lay siege to Jerusalem in 597 B.C. (abused, perhaps, by his captors—see Jeremiah 22:18, 19; 36:30).

Jehoiachin, the king's eighteen-year-old son, quickly surrendered to the Chaldean show of might. This time, Nebuchadnezzar deported to Babylon the king, his wives, the princes of his court, and ten thousand of the nation's best citizens and soldiers—

including Ezekiel, the priest. Once more, he took treasures from the temple (see 2 Kings 24:8-16; Ezekiel 1:1, 2).

As the Egyptian Neco had once dictated who would sit on the throne of Judah, so now the Chaldean Nebuchadnezzar determined the ruler, choosing Zedekiah, another son of Josiah (see 2 Kings 24:17). Like his brother, Zedekiah eventually revolted and brought down upon himself and the nation the wrath of Nebuchadnezzar, resulting in the demolition of the temple, the city of Jerusalem, and the scattering of the captured soldiers and citizens into foreign captivity (see 2 Kings 24:19, 20).

Judah's fate fulfilled the word of the Lord: "Behold, I am bringing upon Jerusalem and Judah such evil that the ears of every one who hears it will tingle. . . . And I will wipe Jerusalem as one wipes a dish, wiping it and turning it upside down" (2 Kings 21:12, 13)!

Spiritual bankruptcy

It would be easy to blame Judah's demise on Josiah's decision to interpose his army into the political vise of the Egyptian-Babylonian power struggle. But the cause of the tragedy lay far deeper. As the prophets Jeremiah and Ezekiel asserted, Judah's collapse resulted from her long-standing love affair with pagan idolatry. The on-again, off-again infatuations had begun in Egypt (see Ezekiel 20 and 23) and had continued through succeeding eras of the judges and the monarchy.

The fifty-five-year reign of Manasseh—forty-four years as sole ruler—engraved the practices of idolatry so deeply in the national consciousness (see Jeremiah 17:1) that it seemed beyond all erasure (see Jeremiah 15:4). The most gross forms of idolatry and spiritualism were widely practiced—even in the temple courts. "Manasseh seduced [Judah] to do more evil than the nations had done whom the Lord destroyed before the people of Israel" (2 Kings 21:9). Even though the king attempted to change the national course near the end of his life (see 2 Chronicles 33:10-19), his reforms had no lasting effect on the people.

In his twelfth year Josiah, Manasseh's grandson, earnestly began to turn the nation around, removing the externals of idolatry from Jerusalem and Judah and from the territories once occupied by the northern kingdom of Israel (see 2 Chronicles 34:3-7). Jeremiah joined Josiah the following year (see Jeremiah 1:2; 25:3), and for the next eighteen years, king and prophet labored together to bring about a genuine reformation.

The discovery of the temple copy of Moses' writings provided a strong impetus to their endeavors, leading to a national assembly and a public commitment to the covenant originally solemnized between the Lord and Israel at Sinai (see 2 Kings 23:1-3). Jeremiah's ministry likewise recalled the nation to the claims and privileges of the covenant relationship (see Jeremiah 11:1-10).

But with the untimely death of Josiah, the reformation swiftly unraveled. Entire families—husbands, wives, and children—engaged in idol worship openly in the streets (see Jeremiah 7:17, 18). Once again, the temple became the site for the practices of idolatrous rites—even by leaders who had formerly associated with Josiah in reforms (see Ezekiel 8:7-12). God revealed to an amazed Jeremiah that the reformation had accomplished only superficial changes. "Judah did not return to me with her whole heart, but in pretense," the Lord said (Jeremiah 3:10).

In the last twenty-two years of Judah's statehood, national leadership (prince, priest, and so-called prophet) as well as citizens became so engrossed in idolatry—shamelessly violating the covenant bond (see Jeremiah 5:20-31)—that the Lord withdrew His protection from the nation. Terrible was the chastisement by its Chaldean foes in combat, siege, and captivity. But the divine promise was that the rigorous discipline would bring about an awakened, penitent remnant. From a seventy-year gestation in Babylon, a new Israel would issue forth (see Jeremiah 29:10-14).

The last kings of Judah

Josiah (639-608 B.C.). Grandson of Manasseh (d. 641 B.C.). Reigned thirty-one years.

Jehoahaz (608 B.C.). Son of Josiah. Reigned three months.

Jehoiakim (608-598 B.C.). Son of Josiah. Reigned eleven years.

Jehoiachin [Jeconiah, Coniah] (598-597 B.C.). Grandson of Josiah. Reigned three months.

Zedekiah (597-586 B.C.). Son of Josiah. Reigned eleven years.

Confirming evidence

Modern archeological discovery and research have both clarified and confirmed many biblical accounts. The book of Jeremiah shares in this illumination too. The most striking piece of information from Jeremiah's time is a statement from the Babylonian Chronicle that tersely summarizes Nebuchadnezzar's conquest of Jerusalem, the capture and deportment of king Jehoiachin, and his replacement with Zedekiah in 597 B.C.:

> [Nebuchadnezzar] encamped against the city of Judah and on the 2d day of the month of Adar he seized the city and captured the king. He appointed there a king of his own choice (lit. "heart"), received its heavy tribute and sent (them) to Babylon.[3]

This ancient record provides Bible students with one of the best attested dates in Old Testament history. The second of Adar in Nebuchadnezzar's seventh regnal year—by our system of chronology—was March 16. But scholarship can be even more precise. March 16 in 597 B.C. was a Saturday. The final assault and capture of Jerusalem took place on the Sabbath![4]

This Sabbath attack is our earliest evidence that alien armies at times deliberately engaged in military strikes against the Jews on their day of worship, fully expecting to find no opposition. Both Ptolemy Soter of Egypt, and still later, the Seleucid armies were to succeed against the Jews by this same ploy. But the Maccabeans abandoned the policy: "Whosoever shall come to make a battle with us on the sabbath day, we will fight against him; neither will we die all, as our brethren" (1 Maccabees 2:41).[5]

Two other bits of information add insight to Nebuchadnezzar's capture of young Jehoiachin. First, clay impressions from a seal containing the inscription "Belonging to Eliakim, steward of Yaukin" have been found in the Palestinian soil. *Yaukin* is a shortened form of *Jehoiachin*.[6] Scholars interpret this data to mean that neither the Babylonians nor Jehoiachin's uncle, Zedekiah, confiscated the young king's estates but permitted his steward to continue their management.

Nebuchadnezzar may have planned to reestablish Jehoiachin on his throne after a period of training in the arts and ways of Babylon. After all, Daniel and his three friends were at that time serving the

Babylonian state, having received three years of instruction in "the letters and language of the Chaldeans" (Daniel 1:4). Nebuchadnezzar could have reasoned that the eighteen-year-old Jehoiachin, with proper guidance and counseling, could become a loyal supporter of the empire, and thus secure the important bridge land of Palestine to the service of the empire. In that case, the door must be left open for Jehoiachin's easy return.

The second item comes from three hundred tablets listing the rations allotted to government dependents for the years 595 to 570 B.C. Among these are tablets dated to 592 B.C. that list the provisions for "king Jehoiachin of Judah," his five sons, and their tutor. This means that five years after his capture, the Babylonians still regarded Jehoiachin as the *king* of Judah, although his uncle Zedekiah sat on the throne.[7]

Excavations at Lachish have recovered twenty-one messages written in ink on broken pieces of pottery (the scratch paper of ancient Palestine) from a field officer to the commander of the Jewish troops in Lachish. We catch the excitement of the conflict against overwhelming forces in the officer's hastily written note: "And let (my lord) know that we are watching for the signals of Lachish, according to all the indications which my Lord hath given, for we cannot see Azekah."[8] One by one the lights of Jewish independence were being extinguished (see Jeremiah 34:7).

Before the Babylonians withdrew from conquered Judah, they appointed Gedaliah, a man of noble descent, as governor over the land (see Jeremiah 40:5). His first task was to pacify the units of the scattered Jewish forces still in the field. A seal containing the name of Jaazaniah has been found in the area of his headquarters. Some scholars believe the seal is to be identified with one of these field officers (of the same name) with whom Gedaliah had to deal. Over the inscription of a fighting cock appear these words: "Jaazaniah, servant of the king"[9] (see 2 Kings 25:23).

Another field captain, Ishmael, of royal blood (see Jeremiah 41:1), was urged by Baalis, king of the Ammonites in Transjoran, to assassinate the new governor (see Jeremiah 40:14). No reason is given, but it is a historical fact that the Ammonites were tied into the Davidic dynasty through Naamah, an Ammonite wife of Solomon and the mother of their son, Rehoboam, the first king of Judah after the division of the monarchy (see 1 Kings 14:21; 2 Chronicles 12:13).

A seal of an Ammonite official, recovered at a 1984 excavation in the Ammonite foothills, dated to ca. 600 B.C., reads: "Belonging to Milkom-ur, servant of Baalis." This seal provides the first extra-biblical confirmation of the Ammonite king Baalis, who plotted the death of Gedaliah.[10]

Archaeological findings color in here and there the larger outlines of the historical setting of Jeremiah's ministry. Such confirmations of the Scriptures assure us that we are reading about the lives of real people—God's chosen people—and their physical and spiritual interaction with the world around them. Living on this side of the Incarnation and in the light that streams from Calvary, we may still profit from a study of Jeremiah's life and forty years of service for God and country.

Distinctive features

The book of Jeremiah is more a compilation of oracles, sermons, autobiographical sketches, and history than a book in our modern sense of the term—with an introduction, development, and conclusion. Furthermore, the writings are not arranged chronologically.

Another difficulty for the modern reader is the lack of a clear-cut topical arrangement, although some scholars perceive a purposeful juxtaposing of certain chapters. For example, chapters 18 and 19 employ pottery as a visual aid. Chapter 18 portrays Judah as clay in the Potter's hand, still capable of being made into a useful vessel, whereas chapter 19 likens Judah to a clay pot (already formed and fired) that is smashed to pieces, beyond mending. Chapter 34 records a covenant that Zedekiah and the princes shamelessly break. Chapter 35 records the experience of the Rechabites, who, for two hundred years, faithfully kept their covenant promise to Jonadab, their ancestor, to never drink wine.

Another feature of Jeremiah's writings is that they appear to have circulated at first in several discrete units. Daniel, for example, refers to the "books" of Jeremiah (see Daniel 9:2). In chapter 30, verse 2, the prophet is told to write a book (usually designated "the book of consolations"), probably chapters 30 and 31. Again, in Jehoiakim's fourth year, Jeremiah is told to write a book that would include all the messages given him from the time he began his ministry to that present time. Because the king destroyed this scroll, it was rewritten, but in more detail (see Jeremiah 36:1, 2, 32). Then there are two letters that Jeremiah wrote to the exiles in

Babylon (see Jeremiah 29:1-32). Scholars see other units.

The fact that the book of Jeremiah is a compilation (along whatever scheme adopted by the compiler—whether the prophet himself or Baruch, his secretary, or another) in no wise affects Jeremiah's essential message given to Judah. Nor will it cause any concern for our present purpose as we propose to examine a few of the large themes that continue to have important significance for modern Christians.

---

1. R. K. Harrison, *Jeremiah and Lamentations. Tyndale Old Testament Commentaries*, ed. D. J. Wiseman (Leicester, England: InterVarsity Press, 1973), 14; Geoffrey W. Bromiley, ed., *The International Standard Bible Encyclopedia*, rev. ed. (Grand Rapids, Mich.: William B. Eerdmans Publishing Co., 1986), 3:470. Hereafter, cited as *ISBE*.

2. This expression is commonly applied to the Bible lands, as they appear to arch in a semicircle from Egypt and the Nile northward through Palestine and Syria and then southward through Mesopotamia (the land between the Euphrates and Tigris rivers) to the Persian Gulf.

3. Siegfried H. Horn, *Seventh-day Adventist Bible Dictionary* (Washington, D.C.: Review and Herald Publishing Association, 1960), s.v. "Jehoiachin," 558. Hereafter cited as *SDABD*.

4. Alger F. Johns, "The Military Strategy of Sabbath Attacks on the Jews," *Vetus Testamentum* (Leiden: E. J. Brill, 1963), 13:483, 484. It may also be determined from the Bible's dateline that Nebuchadnezzar's final siege of Jerusalem—begun on January 15, 588 B.C. (see Jeremiah 52:4)—was a Sabbath day. Ibid., 484.

5. Ibid., 482, 483.

6. *SDABD*, s.v. "Jehoiachin."

7. Ibid.

8. "Lachish Ostracon IV," *Ancient Near Eastern Texts*, 2nd ed., ed. James B. Pritchard (Princeton, N.J.: Princeton University Press, 1955), 322. Hereafter cited as ANET.

9. Werner Keller, *The Bible as History in Pictures* (New York: William Morrow and Company, 1964), 276.

10. Lawrence T. Geraty, "The Andrews University Madaba Plains Project," *Andrews University Seminary Studies* 23 (Spring 1985):98.

Chapter 2
A Prophet's Pilgrimage

One God, one law, one element,
And one far-off divine event,
To which the whole creation moves.[1]

The Scriptures reveal that the Creator rules in the earth according to an "eternal purpose," which He will achieve through Jesus Christ (see Ephesians 3:11). The "eternal purpose" is essentially the outworking of the plan of salvation (in all its varied aspects). This plan the Godhead laid out before earth's creation—an emergency "backup" should the human race rebel against the divine authority.[2]

Each believer has a place and a function in God's overarching purpose (see Romans 8:28, 29). And in the experience of each sinner saved and transformed by divine grace, we see a microcosm of what the Creator desires to do for the entire world. The penitent sinner who responds to the divine call begins a spiritual pilgrimage—growing in grace, knowledge, and experience (see 2 Peter 3:18) as he or she travels toward the eternal kingdom.

Intertwined with his messages and the events of Judah's last forty years of nationhood, Jeremiah sketches his own pilgrimage of faith. Although each believer's experience is unique, we can learn from the prophet's interaction with the challenges that faced him as he strode across the Judean landscape from early youth to old age.

Background and call
Jeremiah's pilgrimage began in a Levitical home. His father, Hilkiah, served as a priest in the temple and nurtured the family in nearby Anathoth, one of the thirteen towns assigned to the

priesthood (see Joshua 21:4, 13-19). Being a descendant of Aaron, Jeremiah was a relative of his much younger contemporary, Ezekiel, who likewise trained for the priesthood (see Ezekiel 1:3).

Since the priests functioned as teachers, expounding the sacred Scriptures (see Malachi 2:7), there is little doubt that the lad received thorough instruction in the religious faith of Israel. His dozen allusions to the *torah* ("the law," God's instructions) indicate a pious home and the training he received in the Mosaic writings.

Jeremiah's familiarity with the temple layout—its courts and chambers—and its personnel suggests that he often accompanied his father to the temple or slipped away on his own to observe the white-robed priests and to ponder the significance of the rituals.

While his life was sheltered and his convictions untried, under the tutelage of godly parents, Hilkiah's son developed an authentic religious experience. His numerous prayers and meditations indicate that the young man began early to talk to God as to a Friend. It was this habit of "discussing" with God his observations, complaints, questions, and doubts—openly and freely—that kept the prophet in his moments of discouragement from abandoning his calling.

Jeremiah received his call to the prophetic ministry in a state of vision. "Before I formed you in the womb I knew you, and before you were born I consecrated you; I appointed you a prophet to the nations," the Lord announced to the amazed young man (Jeremiah 1:5). The omniscient God had planned Jeremiah's part in His eternal purpose long before he was conceived! Here is a striking example of the divine initiative in human affairs.[3]

Actually God had already anticipated this moment three hundred years earlier. Through an anonymous prophet He had announced to the startled Jeroboam I, king of the newly formed nation of Israel, that a ruler of the Davidic dynasty, Josiah by name, would destroy the idolatrous worship the king was inaugurating at Bethel (see 1 Kings 13:1-3). By 626 B.C. Josiah had been on the throne for thirteen years and was already engaged in smashing the idol shrines in both Judah and the nearby territories of the former kingdom of Israel, including the Bethel shrine (see 2 Chronicles 34:1-7; 2 Kings 23:15-20). Now, God summoned Jeremiah to join King Josiah in a final attempt to turn the apostate nation around.

If God had a specific role for Jeremiah and Josiah in His eternal purpose, does He not have one for each of us? The divine omniscience is beyond our human comprehension; we scarcely can grasp the idea. But if the Creator has a place and name for every star glowing in the heavens (see Isaiah 40:26; Psalm 147:3-5), He surely has a place and purpose for each of His followers in the grand design of salvation!

The highly educated, eighty-year-old Moses (see Acts 7:22) gave a series of excuses why he shouldn't accept God's call to lead Israel from Egypt (see Exodus 3:10–4:17). Isaiah was overwhelmed by his sinfulness (see Isaiah 6:1-8). But the youthful, self-effacing Jeremiah spoke only the truth when he responded: "Ah, Lord God! Behold, I do not know how to speak, for I am only a youth" (Jeremiah 1:6). But the Lord brushed aside his protest.

God delights to employ the insignificant to accomplish His purpose (see 1 Corinthians 1:27-29). In the vision, as Jeremiah later recorded, "The Lord put forth his hand and touched my mouth; and . . . said to me, 'Behold, I have put my words in your mouth. See, I have set you this day over nations and over kingdoms, to pluck up and to break down, to destroy and to overthrow, to build and to plant' " (Jeremiah 1:9, 10).

Now the priest-in-training, possibly twenty- to twenty-five years old and not yet serving in the temple (see Numbers 4:3; 1 Chronicles 23:3), acquiesces in silence. Immediately he is given, as it were, a short course in comprehending prophetic visions! A flowering almond branch appears before his inner sight. "Jeremiah, what do you see?"

"I see a rod of almond," the young man replies.

"You have seen well, for I am watching over my word to perform it," announces the Lord (Jeremiah 1:11, 12).

From his priestly connection with the temple, Jeremiah would have been well acquainted with the symbolism of the almond. The menorah—the golden, seven-branched lampstand with its continuously burning lamps located in the first apartment, was a stylized almond tree (see Exodus 25:31-39; Leviticus 24:1-4). The almond was called a "watch" or "wake" (Hebrew *shāqēd*) tree because it bloomed earliest in the new growing season. God made a play on the almond's name: "You have seen well, for I am *watching* [Hebrew *shōqēd*] over my word to perform it" (Jeremiah 1:12).

The symbolism of the almond (and possibly its connection with the continuously burning menorah in the temple) underscored to the young prophet the falsity of the current attitudes held by

Judah's intelligentsia: "The Lord does not see us, the Lord has forsaken the land" (Ezekiel 8:12). On the contrary, the Lord was awake, alert, watching—about to break into Judah's complacency. Long had judgment been delayed for the sinful nation. Now, a sure and speedy fulfillment could be expected.

Again, a representation appears before the prophet, and the divine Inquirer asks, "What do you see?"

"I see a boiling pot, facing away from the north," Jeremiah replies (Jeremiah 1:13). The pot, tipped southward toward Judah, is about to spill its scalding retribution.

With her borders secured on the east by the Arabian Desert and on the west by the Mediterranean Sea, Palestine's military attacks came either from the south (Egypt) or from the north. "Out of the north," the Lord explained to Jeremiah, "evil shall break forth upon all the inhabitants of the land. . . . And I will utter my judgments against them, for all their wickedness in forsaking me" (Jeremiah 1:14-16).

Divine patience had reached its limits. The people of Judah, for the most part, were incorrigible. In voicing God's appeal, Jeremiah would be met with sullen hostility, but he was not to back down nor be discouraged. "I make you this day a fortified city, an iron pillar, and bronze walls, against . . . the kings of Judah, its princes, its priests, and the people of the land," the Lord assured, "but they shall not prevail against you, for I am with you . . . to deliver you" (Jeremiah 1:18, 19).

A sensitive personality

Did the Lord make a mistake in transforming a warmhearted, sympathetic youth into "a fortified city, an iron pillar, and bronze walls" kind of person? Although at times he cried out for retribution on his persecutors, the prophet never lost his compassionate nature. An early vision, portraying the approaching national ruin, devastated him: "My anguish, my anguish! I writhe in pain! Oh, the walls of my heart! My heart is beating wildly; I cannot keep silent; for I hear the sound of the trumpet, the alarm of war" (Jeremiah 4:19).

Pain and disappointment sometimes harden our attitude against those who at first excite pity, but who persistently refuse our help. But even at the midpoint of Jeremiah's ministry—matured and seasoned—he continued to feel deeply over the wayward nation.

The prophet's genuine sensitivity prevented him from merely scolding or shouting.

> My grief is beyond healing, my heart is sick within me. . . . For the wound of the daughter of my people is my heart wounded, I mourn, and dismay has taken hold on me. Is there no balm in Gilead? Is there no physician there? Why then has the health of the daughter of my people not been restored? O that my head were waters, and my eyes a fountain of tears, that I might weep day and night for the slain of the daughter of my people! (Jeremiah 8:18–9:1).

Jeremiah's lament—reflecting the divine pathos—is like "a heart-sickness of a betrayed lover or a yearning parent. One sees the trouble of the lover or child, wants to head it off, but must stand helplessly while the disease works to its dread conclusion of death."[4]

Even in his final pronouncements against his beloved nation, the derided and abused prophet still weeps for the people: "Hear and give ear; be not proud, for the Lord has spoken. . . . But if you will not listen, my soul will weep in secret for your pride; my eyes will weep bitterly and run down with tears, because the Lord's flock has been taken captive" (Jeremiah 13:15-17). If you will not weep for yourselves, I will weep for you, he exclaims, in effect!

The tears of the servant prophet anticipated those of his Master, who would weep over another disobedient generation of His people (see Luke 19:41, 42). Neither Jesus nor Jeremiah withdrew the proffered grace. But the indifferent and hostile rulers and people with haughty self-sufficiency knocked aside the hand outstretched to save!

Suffering for God's sake

The halcyon years under King Josiah suddenly terminated for the prophet when his patron and protector died, and Pharaoh Neco appointed Jehoiakim to the throne. Throughout his eighteen years with Josiah, Jeremiah's reproofs and appeals had been addressed to the religious and civil leaders, as well as to the general citizens. Now their suppressed anger exploded upon the unsuspecting prophet.

A violent reaction followed his Temple Sermon in which he predicted the ruin of temple and city (see Jeremiah 7:1-5; 26:1-24).[5]

Infuriated priests, false prophets, and people accused Jeremiah before the princes, who had hastily assembled at one of the temple gates. "This man deserves the sentence of death, because he has prophesied against this city, as you have heard with your own ears," they angrily shouted (Jeremiah 26:11).

The prophet surveyed the faces contorted with fury, then calmly explained:

> The Lord sent me to prophesy against this house and this city all the words you have heard. . . . I am in your hands. Do with me as seems good and right to you. Only know for certain that if you put me to death, you will bring innocent blood upon yourselves and upon this city and its inhabitants, for in truth the Lord sent me to speak all these words in your ears (verses 12-15).

On this occasion the princes pacified the people and rescued Jeremiah from the wrath of the priests and people (see Jeremiah 26:16, 24).

Fearless before the incensed crowd in the temple, Jeremiah nevertheless was overwhelmed by a revelation from God that his neighbors in Anathoth plotted his death, abetted by his own brothers and relatives (see Jeremiah 11:18, 19; 12:6)! "I was like a gentle lamb led to the slaughter. I did not know it was against me they devised schemes," he exclaimed (Jeremiah 11:19). As conditions worsened with the passing years, such plots on his life surfaced from time to time (see Jeremiah 18:18-23; 38:4).

Like the Saviour, Jeremiah never publicly reviled or threatened his enemies, who thirsted for his blood (see 1 Peter 2:23). But in his prayers—unlike Jesus—he poured out his pain and anger, appealing for vindication: "Let me see thy vengeance upon them" (Jeremiah 11:20; see especially 18:19-23).

Jeremiah's spiritual pilgrimage had not reached the point where he could pray for his enemies, as did Jesus and Stephen: "Father, forgive them; for they know not what they do" (Luke 23:34; see also Acts 7:60).

In addition to plots on his life, God's faithful witness endured the daily mocking and derision of the people, a flogging at the hand of one of the priests, and a night of torture in the stocks,[6] as well as imprisonments (see Jeremiah 20:1-7; 37:15).

During the final siege of Jerusalem, the princes accused the prophet of treason and demanded his death (see Jeremiah 38:1-4). The vacillating Zedekiah yielded to their urging, and Jeremiah was lowered into a muddy cistern to die of starvation. Only the compassion and boldness of an Ethiopian servant in the king's palace saved the prophet from a lingering death (see verses 7-13).

But even in the face of a violent death, Jeremiah never broke, never surrendered his integrity. And God fulfilled His promise: "I will deliver you out of the hand of the wicked, and redeem you from the grasp of the ruthless" (Jeremiah 15:21).

Fighting depression and despondency

While presenting a consistent public image as God's spokesman, Jeremiah was not always at peace with himself. Doubts and perplexities regarding God's dealings with Judah tormented him at times. Forbidden to marry and to rear a family—because his private life was also to enforce his public witness of imminent doom (see Jeremiah 16:1-9)—Jeremiah had no close companion with whom he could share his concerns and feelings.

The persistent obstinacy of the people and the hopelessness of his ministry drove him to despair. Twice he contemplated abandoning his commission altogether. The prophet never disclosed his doubts to the people, but he "discussed" and aired his "complaints" with God. In this respect, he set a worthy example for all God's representatives.

Jeremiah, chapters 12 to 20, are sometimes described as "The Confessions of Jeremiah," because they record the inward struggles of God's servant. Like Job, depression dogged him, and on occasion he gave expression to his dark thoughts:

> Cursed be the day on which I was born! . . . Cursed be the man who brought the news to my father, 'A son is born to you,' making him very glad. Let that man be like the cities which the Lord overthrew without pity (Jeremiah 20:14-16).

The nadir of his distress was produced by the troubling thought that the God he so earnestly served was not trustworthy or dependable. "Why is my pain unceasing, my wound incurable, refusing to be healed? *Wilt thou be to me like a deceitful brook, like waters that fail?*" (Jeremiah 15:18, emphasis added).

Here the prophet probably refers to the Palestinian wadi, a valley through which water flows in the rainy season, but which dries up during the rest of the year. Is the God he serves like a wadi, sometimes full, sometimes empty? Sometimes present to save? At other times apparently absent, silent, or indifferent?

Jeremiah doesn't explain why he questions God's reliability. And the Lord doesn't argue with His perplexed prophet. He simply says, "If you return, I will restore you, and you shall stand before me," and assures him once more that He will enable Jeremiah to withstand his enemies (see Jeremiah 15:19-21).

Once more, after a flogging and a night in the stocks, the prophet reached a low point and groaned out his prayer: "O Lord, thou hast deceived me, and I was deceived; thou art stronger than I, and thou hast prevailed. I have become a laughingstock all the day; every one mocks me" (Jeremiah 20:7). He considered quitting again but could not rid himself of the divine compulsion to discharge God's orders: "If I say, 'I will not mention him, nor speak any more in his name,' there is in my heart as it were a burning fire shut up in my bones, and I am weary with holding it in, and I cannot" (verse 9).

But this time, Jeremiah's faith grasped God's previous promises to help him discharge his commission. He soliloquized in his prayer: "The Lord is with me as a dread warrior; therefore my persecutors will stumble, they will not overcome me. They will be greatly shamed, for they will not succeed. Their eternal dishonor will never be forgotten" (verse 11).

When Jeremiah was informed that the men of Anathoth plotted his assassination, he was prompted to ask a question that had long been bubbling within. With fitting deference, he prayed: "Righteous art thou, O Lord, when I complain to thee; yet I would plead my case before thee." Then came the troubling question, asked in every generation: "Why does the way of the wicked prosper? Why do all who are treacherous thrive?" (Jeremiah 12:1).

Jeremiah's problem was a case of self-pity. He knew the answer to his own query. He needed only to read again Asaph's psalm (Psalm 73), written by the famous temple singer, whose psalms— as a priest-in-training—he had doubtlessly read and sung. God doesn't argue with him but simply says: "If you have raced with men on foot, and they have wearied you, how will you compete with horses? And if in a safe land you fall down, how will you do in the jungle of the Jordan?" (Jeremiah 12:5). It was as if God were restating a proverb of Solomon: "If you faint in the day of adversity, your strength is small" (Proverbs 24:10). Jeremiah accepted the gentle, though unvarnished reproof. It would take the years of his ministry to adapt to its implications.

Jeremiah could not doubt but that larger issues and challenges would face him in the future. But each small step he took successfully in his spiritual pilgrimage would enable him to take more certain strides in the future. The prophet's experience stands as a testimony that an innocent, but untested faith, battered by the white-water rapids of life, can become, under divine grace, a deep and knowledgeable trust, settled and fixed on the promises of the eternal God. Jeremiah nobly filled his place in God's eternal purpose.

---

1. Alfred Lord Tennyson, "In Memoriam," cited in *The Oxford Dictionary of Quotations*, 2nd ed. (London: Oxford University Press, 1955), 533, line 31.

2. See Matthew 25:34, 41; Romans 16:25, 26; 1 Corinthians 2:7; Ephesians 1:3-5; Titus 1:2; 2 Timothy 1:9, 10; 1 Peter 1:18-20.

3. For a brief discussion on how God "rules" in human affairs, see Francis D. Nichol, ed., *Seventh-day Adventist Bible Commentary* (Washington, D.C.: Review and Herald Publishing Association, 1977), 4:790, 791. Hereafter cited as SDABC.

4. Walter Brueggemann, *To Pluck Up, to Tear Down—A Commentary on the Book of Jeremiah 1-25, International Theological Commentary*, ed. Frederick C. Holmgren, George A. F. Knight (Grand Rapids, Mich.: Wm. B. Eerdmans Publishing Co., 1988), 88.

5. The two passages are thought to deal with the same address, the latter describing the reaction. See R. K. Harrison, *Jeremiah and Lamentations*, 85.

6. "The Hebrew word is formed from the verb to twist, implying that this 'twist-frame' clamped the victim in a position that would become increasingly distressing" (Derek Kidner, *The Message of Jeremiah, The Bible Speaks Today* series, ed. J. A. Motyer, [Downers Grove, Ill.: Inter-Varsity Press, 1987], 79).

Chapter 3
No Other God

Seated on the summit of a high mountain, the sun warm on His back, the Master gazed upon the shimmering valley far below. Suddenly, a giant, demonic video began to roll—scenes of faraway places took shape on the valley floor. Cities teeming with happy people, lordly palaces and noble mansions, glistening rivers flowing through cattle-covered hills and broad plains, lush croplands, and fruit-laden orchards appeared before His eyes. Kings, queens, and courtiers of famous and favored lands silently moved across the living screen. In a moment of time, as it were, He saw "all the kingdoms of the world and the glory of them."

As the colorful mirage swept past, Satan challenged the Master's motives: "All these I will give you, if you will fall down and worship me," he offered. Christ had come at great cost to win the revolted planet back to God. Now, the usurper offered an easier means for obtaining the desired end: simply acknowledge Satan's supremacy and lordship. Quickly, the Master turned on the foe of all righteousness: "Begone, Satan! for it is written, 'You shall worship the Lord your God and him only shall you serve' " (Matthew 4:8-10).

A fundamental truth

Christ's forthright declaration reaffirmed an absolute truth, the cornerstone of biblical religion: there is only one sovereign Deity—the triune God—to whom all created intelligences in the broad universe owe their allegiance and devotion. The Master cited the essence of Deuteronomy 6:13 and 10:20 from the same "book of the law" that served as the basis for Josiah's reforms and Jeremiah's appeals to the idol-enthralled people of Judah.

A few days before His crucifixion, Jesus restated this fundamental truth in reply to the question: "Which commandment is the first of all?" Again, He turned to the book of Deuteronomy: "The first is, 'Hear, O Israel: The Lord our God, the Lord is one; and you shall love the Lord your God with all your heart, and with all your soul, and with all your mind, and with all your strength' " (Mark 12:29, 30, citing Deuteronomy 6:4, 5).

The moral law of the Ten Commandments, the principles of which form the "constitution" of the divine government, addresses the reality that there is only one true God by forbidding the worship of any other claimant. "You shall have no other gods before me" (Exodus 20:3). On its positive side, the precept means that every intelligent being will voluntarily give first place in his or her affections and obedience to the God of Creation, who is revealed in the Scriptures. All other precepts of the moral law flow from this foundational truth. The three commands that follow instruct how humans shall worship, respect, and honor the true God; the last six precepts—the second table of the law—define how they shall relate to one another, for all are the children of His creative hand.

The reason wholehearted allegiance to the triune God is the Bible's fundamental truth is that God is the Creator, the Source of all life. Just as parents may rightfully expect the obedience of their children, so the Creator expects the allegiance of His creation. "Worthy art thou, our Lord and God," praise the inhabitants of heaven, "to receive glory and honor and power, for thou didst create all things, and by thy will they existed and were created" (Revelation 4:11).

Judah's long-standing affair

The descendants of Jacob had an on-again, off-again flirtation with idolatrous worship ever since their extended exposure to it in Egypt (see Ezekiel 20:6-8). But during Judah's last fifty years of statehood, its abandonment to full-blown idolatry was practically universal. A strange amnesia erased their remembrance of the first precept of the Decalogue, spoken by the Creator Himself and recorded with His own finger on the tables of stone kept in the temple.

With an air of surprised innocence the people scarcely credited Jeremiah's announcement of divine judgment on the nation. "Why has the Lord pronounced all this great evil against us? What is our iniquity? What is the sin that we have committed against the Lord our God?" they inquire. Give them this reply, the Lord instructed

Jeremiah: "Because your fathers have forsaken me, says the Lord, and have gone after other gods and have served and worshiped them, and have forsaken me and have not kept my law, and because you have done worse than your fathers" (Jeremiah 16:10-12; see also chapter 22:8, 9).

What seemed hidden to the conscience-blinded Jews was obvious to the foreign visitor to their cities and capital. Every town had its patron god or goddess, and every street in Jerusalem had its smoking-incense altar (see Jeremiah 11:13; 2:28). Entire families engaged in the worship of astral deities such as the queen of heaven (usually identified with the Assyrian-Babylonian Ishtar, a fertility goddess of sexual love and war). "Do you not see what they are doing in the cities of Judah and in the streets of Jerusalem?" the Lord asked Jeremiah. "The children gather wood, the fathers kindle fire, and the women knead dough, to make cakes for the queen of heaven; and they pour out drink offerings to other gods, to provoke me to anger" (Jeremiah 7:17, 18).

Judah's love affair with pagan idolatry did more than simply displace God from the center of its affections. Idolatry inevitably degrades and demeans its devotees. If we do not worship the true Creator who is above us, we will eventually grovel before that which is beneath us. There was a dark side to Judah's idolatry. One aspect was its gross licentiousness (see Isaiah 57:5). Cultic prostitution was prominent (see Hosea 4:14; Numbers 25:1, 2; see also Revelation 2:14). So was human sacrifice.

God indicted Judah in strong terms: "The people have forsaken me, . . . they have filled this place with the blood of innocents, and have built the high places of Baal to burn their sons in the fire as burnt offerings to Baal, which I did not command or decree, nor did it come into my mind" (Jeremiah 19:4, 5; see also chapter 7:31). In the same valley of the son of Hinnom, south of Jerusalem, the Jews also worshiped Molech, the god of the Ammonites, devoting their children "by fire" to the idol (see Leviticus 18:21; Jeremiah 32:34, 35). Some have thought that the "sacrifice" consisted of passing the child quickly through the flame, withdrawing it alive. But the site for these cruel rites is described by the Hebrew word *tophet*, the probable root of which means "fireplace" or "incinerator" (see Jeremiah 7:31; 19:6). There is little doubt that the Molech cult worship involved the cremation of human victims (see Ezekiel 16:20, 21).[1]

Beyond the crudities of image veneration, the immoralities of sensual rites, and the sacrificial murder of innocent children appears the real heart of pagan idolatry: the worship of demons—Satan and the fallen angels. The psalmist speaks clearly: "They served their idols. . . . They sacrificed their sons and their daughters to the demons; they poured out innocent blood, the blood of their sons and daughters, whom they sacrificed to the idols of Canaan" (Psalm 106:36-38; compare 1 Corinthians 10:20, 21).

Oddly enough, Judah's passionate pursuit of idolatry did not in the least close down the rituals and liturgy of the temple. The Jews were proud of the temple of Yahweh and believed it would stand forever, in spite of Jeremiah's warning to the contrary. "Do not trust in these deceptive words," he appealed. "This is the temple of the Lord, the temple of the Lord, the temple of the Lord" (Jeremiah 7:4). Judah developed a syncretistic religious lifestyle. The courts of the temple were packed with worshipers who at the same time embraced the worship of other gods. The Lord called attention to this impossible stance through both Ezekiel and Jeremiah: "This they have done to me: they have defiled my sanctuary on the same day and profaned my sabbaths. For when they had slaughtered their children in sacrifice to their idols, on the same day they came into my sanctuary to profane it" (Ezekiel 23:38, 39). "Behold, you trust in deceptive words to no avail. Will you . . . burn incense to Baal, and go after other gods that you have not known, and then come and stand before me in this house, which is called by my name, and say, 'We are delivered!'—only to go on doing all these abominations?" (Jeremiah 7:8-10).

Truly, "the god of this world"—Satan—had blinded the minds of God's ancient people. "No servant can serve two masters" is an ancient truth (Luke 16:13). What Christ would later reject in Satan's third temptation, Judah attempted to clasp to her bosom: the service of Yahweh combined with the service of the pagan pantheons. In reality, their allegiance to the true God was totally displaced. The divine astonishment cannot find in comparison any such abandonment of even false deities in the world community:

> Cross to the coasts of Cyprus [westward] and see, or send to Kedar [eastward] and examine with care; see if there has been such a thing. Has a nation changed its gods, even though they are no gods? But my people have changed their glory for that which does not profit. . . . They have forsaken me, the foun-

tain of living waters, and hewed out cisterns for themselves, broken cisterns, that can hold no water (Jeremiah 2:10-13).

Collapsing morality

The religion of the Bible revolves around two centers: supreme love to God and impartial love to fellow beings (see Matthew 22: 35-40). When respect for God fades, respect for people fades as well. Self-love and self-centeredness take control, and soon the whole range of sins against others permeates society.

In order to convince Jeremiah of the depraved condition of the nation, God ordered him: "Run to and fro through the streets of Jerusalem, look and take note! Search her squares to see if you can find a man, one who does justice and seeks truth; that I may pardon her" (Jeremiah 5:1). Among the common people he found only stubborn refusal to accept divine "correction." Unsuccessful there, the prophet turned to the intelligentsia. But his search was again fruitless; he was forced to admit that they too had broken away from their covenant relationship with God (see Jeremiah 5:5).

The very fabric of the society was being rent asunder. Mutual trust no longer existed. Being false to God, leaders and people were fast becoming false to one another (see Jeremiah 9:3). "Let every one beware of his neighbor, and put no trust in any brother" (Jeremiah 9:4). They had schooled themselves to lie and were too weary to resolve the resultant entanglements. "Every one deceives his neighbor, and no one speaks the truth; they have taught their tongue to speak lies; they commit iniquity and are too weary to repent" (verse 5).

Stealing, murder, and adultery were openly practiced (see Jeremiah 7:9). Clients shamelessly crowded the houses of prostitution (see Jeremiah 5:7). Solemn covenants were easily broken if circumstances changed (see Jeremiah 34:8-11). Exploitation and oppression of the widow, the orphan, and the needy were common; their rights were ignored. The prophet was instructed to appeal to the monarchy to execute justice for the oppressed (see Jeremiah 5: 26-28; 21:11, 12). "Do no wrong or violence to the alien, the fatherless, and the widow, nor shed innocent blood in this place," he pleaded (see Jeremiah 22:3).

Greed and the lust for material wealth—dishonestly gained or not—rippled through both the religious and secular communities. "From the least to the greatest of them," declared the Lord, "every one is greedy for unjust gain; and from prophet to priest, every one deals falsely" (Jeremiah 6:13; see also chapter 8:10). If it served the building interests of King Jehoiakim, he withheld the wages of his workmen without any concern for their welfare (see Jeremiah 22:13-18). Law and order ceased to exist.

In the last years of Judah's independence, its subjects became so bold and hardened in their sinful lifestyles that God would ask and answer His own question: "Were they ashamed when they committed abomination? No, they were not at all ashamed; they did not know how to blush" (Jeremiah 6:15).

The most amazing feature of this ruined society, in which civil and religious leaders were openly corrupt and in which life, limb, and property were at risk, was that the people desired nothing better. Wanting no restraint, they were content to sin and to be sinned against! (Jeremiah 5:30, 31).

Message for moderns

Modern people wonder how the ancients could venerate idols of wood and stone or precious metal. They forget that idolatry is more a matter of the inward heart than it is of outward images and visible rites. Because we are sinners by nature (see Ephesians 2:3) and are carnal minded (see Romans 7:14), our false "gods" are always extensions of our sinful selves. And if we give our false "gods" visible form, we simply make them larger-than-life sinners.

What is an idol? The Creator-God has said, "Thou shalt have no other gods before me" (Exodus 20:3, KJV). From the Bible's standpoint, anything that displaces God from the believer's affections and obedience—or interferes with the service due Him—is an idol.[2] And it is easy for sinful humans to place their wills above the will of the Creator. It is the natural autonomy of sinners to be independent of God, to carry out their own desires rather than His.

Are not the men and women of the twentieth century "lovers of pleasure rather than lovers of God" (2 Timothy 3:4)? In lands of affluence, do we not erect our "temples" for sports, races, and amusements? We may not venerate images of Venus and Bacchus, but who can deny that millions worship at the multiple shrines of illicit sex, drinking, and pleasurable escapes through chemical abuse?

Others seek more "refined" gods and worship at the altars of science and humanism. Materialism and mammon occupy the attention of millions; still others are attracted to the goddess of fashion and adornment. Many continue to worship Mars and Ashur under the guise of militarism; and nationalism is the full-time pursuit of other millions. For many there is no true Creator-God at all. The God of the Holy Scriptures, the Father of our Lord Christ, is denied outright. Such often worship at the shrine of atheistic evolutionism. The objects of worship vary, but worship we will!

In reality, these expressions of our "worship" extend the "idols" of our own minds, leaving no room for the Creator and Redeemer of Holy Scripture. Even our stubborn opinions, if they displace God, are a form of idolatry called self-worship. "Stubbornness is as iniquity and idolatry," Samuel declared to King Saul (1 Samuel 15:23). And the basic sin of covetousness, another form of self-worship, is also declared in the Word of God to be "idolatry" (see Colossians 3:5; Ephesians 5:5). Since the Fall of humankind into sin, idolatry in one form or another has always been the basic sin of every age wherever humans do "not see fit to acknowledge God" (Romans 1:28).

Fear, folly, or fidelity

But the creature cannot with impunity abandon the Creator without sad results. We really do not "break" the great principles of either physical or moral law that God designed for human happiness—our violations break us. When we reject the authority of God, we turn away from the very Source of true peace and security, and our violations destroy us. "The way of the transgressor is hard" (Proverbs 13:15, KJV).

Pagan idolatry deified the awesome forces of nature, worshiped the alleged spirits of the dead, and did obeisance to the devils themselves. Astral and terrestrial deities abounded. To personify such unpredictable powers places the idolater under slavery to fear. Then worship degenerates into attempts either to humor or appease the gods lest they become angry and harm their devotees.

Jeremiah appealed to the people to free themselves from their self-inflicted apprehensions and superstitions. "Learn not the way of the nations, nor be dismayed at the signs of the heavens because the nations are dismayed at them, for the customs of the people are false" (Jeremiah 10:2, 3).[3]

Astrology flourished in the Near East, even as it does today in the modern world. Eclipses of the sun and moon, comets, conjunctions of the planets—any celestial phenomenon was viewed as an omen of good or ill, influencing political decisions as well as individual lives. Instead of being stewards of the earth and its life, as the Creator originally designed (see Genesis 1:26, 28), the Jewish idolaters became victims of the powers that they falsely attributed to the natural world.

Like Isaiah in the previous century, Jeremiah satirizes Judah's inordinate infatuation and folly. "Idols are like scarecrows in a cucumber field," he scoffs. "They cannot speak; they have to be carried, for they cannot walk. *Be not afraid of them*, for they cannot do evil, neither is it in them to do good" (Jeremiah 10:5, emphasis added; compare Isaiah 44:19).

We smile at the incredulity of the pagan, but is the modern idolater really wiser when he turns from the God revealed in Scripture, whom he regards as a myth, a vestige from primitive ages? Will his god of humanism, materialism, or hedonism give him any genuine comfort on his deathbed? According to the Scriptures, he is playing games with his most precious commodity—life itself. "It is appointed for men to die once, and after that comes judgment" (Hebrews 9:27).

Jeremiah, however, does more than chide Judah for its fears and follies. He contrasts the helplessness of human gods with the omnipotence of the true God. With broad strokes he portrays the attributes of the only God: "The Lord [Yahweh] is the *true* God; he is the *living* God and the *everlasting* King. At his wrath [judgment] the earth quakes, and the nations cannot endure his indignation. . . . It is he *who made the earth* by his power . . . and . . . *stretched out the heavens*." "The *Lord of hosts* is his name" (Jeremiah 10:10-12, 16, emphasis added).

The true God—the God revealed in the Scriptures—is genuine, faithful, dependable, keeping covenant with those who trust and obey Him (see Deuteronomy 7:9). He is awake and attentive to the supplications of His people. He is the eternal Ruler of the universe. He was here before the entrance of sin and the defection of angels and humans, and He will continue to reign long after the defectors and their idols have perished. He is the Creator of all intelligent beings, and He is their judge. All the forces of the universe are in His hands.

Jeremiah's message (see Jeremiah 10:1-16) implicitly demanded a decision.[4] Would the fear and folly of idol worship control the lives of the Judaists, or would they again be moved to fear the Lord, their Creator and Redeemer, whose steadfast love yearned to embrace them once more as "his own possession" (see Deuteronomy 7:6-11)? Will we, who also are prone to idolatry, make this petition to our Creator and Redeemer?

> The dearest idol I have known,
> Whate'er that idol be,
> Help me to tear it from Thy throne,
> And worship only Thee.[5]

1. *ISBE*, 3:401.
2. Ellen G. White, *Patriarchs and Prophets* (Boise, Idaho: Pacific Press Publishing Association, 1958), 305; *Testimonies for the Church* (Boise, Idaho: Pacific Press Publishing Association, 1948), 1:289; 5:250.
3. K. N. Taylor's paraphrase reminds us that the ancient superstitions are still alive and well in the twentieth century! "Don't act like the people who make horoscopes and try to read their fate and future in the stars! Don't be frightened by predictions such as theirs, for it is all a pack of lies" (Jeremiah 10:2, 3, TLB).
4. Brueggemann, *To Pluck Up, to Tear Down*, 100.
5. William Cowper, "O for a Closer Walk," *The Seventh-day Adventist Hymnal* (Washington, D.C.: Review and Herald Publishing Association, 1985), no. 315.

Chapter 4

Wedding Vows

Battered and scarred, the old leather suitcase stands among the moving boxes. Its brown sides and straps are worn white on the corners and edges; the once-shiny buckles have dulled. Its presence on the porch signals another transfer for its owner.

In move after move, new places and situations, new challenges, the case is never left behind. It has jolted hundred of miles, along with other baggage, in conference or commercial vans. Seldom opened, yet highly prized, the old leather case is carefully stored in the owner's closet at each new location.

Though of medium size, the suitcase contains only one item: a wedding gown! The wear and tear of forty-three years have taken their toll on the crumbling leather case, but the simple white gown, yellowed by time, continues to be cherished.

We smile with understanding at the sentimental regard a wife has for her wedding attire. But what would we think if the yellowing fabric were more precious to her than the husband to whom she pledged her fidelity? Yet, that strange twist had occurred in Judah's relationship with God. We sense the poignancy in God's heartbreaking cry over "the spiritual promiscuity" of Judah, His "runaway bride."[1] "Can a maiden forget her ornaments, or a bride her attire? Yet my people have forgotten me days without number" (Jeremiah 2:32).

A violated marriage

The fundamental charge against both Israel and Judah was not mere forgetfulness, but national adultery! "I remember the devotion of your youth," God recalls, "your love as a bride" (Jeremiah 2:2). But "long ago you broke your yoke and burst your bonds; and

35

you said, 'I will not serve.' Yea, upon every high hill and under every green tree you bowed down as a harlot" (verse 20). Judah's warm affection for God had cooled; she now regarded the relationship as a galling yoke. She "wanted out."

Perhaps God intended to jolt His people into an awareness of their critical situation by alluding to the Mosaic legislation on divorce (see Deuteronomy 24:1-4). "If a man divorces his wife and she goes from him and becomes another man's wife, will he return to her? Would not that land be greatly polluted? You have played the harlot with many lovers; and would you return to me? says the Lord" (Jeremiah 3:1).

The Lord was Judah's first "husband"; pagan gods were represented as her second. If God were governed by Judah's societal codes, the answer to His question would be No. And God wanted His people to realize how desperate their condition was. Nevertheless, the bond between human beings and the Creator is essentially a spiritual one. And it is evident from the thrust of these early chapters in the book that the divine Husband yearned to embrace His people once more, if only they would repent and acknowledge their breach of promise (see Jeremiah 3:12-14; 7:1-3). But Judah was hardened and completely satisfied with her "freedom." And the Lord lamented, "You have polluted the land with your vile harlotry. . . . You have a harlot's brow, you refuse to be ashamed" (Jeremiah 3:2, 3).

The Lord took another approach to arouse Judah. He held up before the nation the experience and fate of her "sister," the northern kingdom of Israel. Israel's first king, Jeroboam I (931-910 B.C.), had introduced his own system of religion (see 1 Kings 12:25-33). This royal nudge toward idolatry combined with their geographical location, which readily allowed cultural and commercial interaction with Phoenicia, Syria, and Assyria, provided an easy entrance for pagan beliefs and practices into the national life. Ahab's marriage to Jezebel, the daughter of Ethbaal, king of the Zidonians, simply opened the floodgates leading to her ruin.

But Judah's dalliance with idolatry was more abhorrent than Israel's. Although Judah saw Israel's disgrace and ruin, she ignored it. "Her false sister Judah did not fear, but she too went and played the harlot. Because harlotry was so light to her, she polluted the land, committing adultery with stone and tree" (Jeremiah 3:8, 9).

At the same time, however, Judah maintained the worship of Yahweh in the temple and appeared to cooperate with Josiah's reforms. But God read the "heart" of the nation: "Yet for all this her false sister Judah did not return to me with her whole heart, but in pretense," He affirmed (verse 10).

Three times in this brief comparison God described Israel as "faithless," but four times He sharply designated Judah as "false" (verses 6-11). Both were guilty of gross infidelity, but the latter openly transgressed against greater light. It is no wonder God flings out an agonizing question to anyone who will listen: "What right has my beloved in my house, when she has done vile deeds?" (Jeremiah 11:15).

The marriage covenant

Readers unfamiliar with Scripture language may wonder why the idolatry of Israel and Judah is described in the shameful terms of adultery and prostitution. The answer is that God regarded His relationship with them as a marriage. "I was their husband, says the Lord" (Jeremiah 31:32); "surely, as a faithless wife leaves her husband, so have you been faithless to me, O house of Israel, says the Lord" (Jeremiah 3:20).

In modern Western society, many couples live together without the benefit of marriage. No commitment binds them. Unwittingly, perhaps, many nominal Christians have a similar relationship with God, calling on Him only when in serious need. But the true religion of the Bible differs from these casual relationships. Behind the spiritual marriage between God and the believer lies a *covenant*, a serious, wholehearted commitment of both parties, divine and human, to each other. When a believer breaks covenant with God, he commits spiritual adultery.

The Lord describes the process of organizing Israel into a nation at Sinai in terms of a marriage covenant. "Behold, you were at the age for love; and I spread my skirt over you, . . . yea, *I plighted my troth to you and entered into a covenant with you*, says the Lord God, *and you became mine*" (Ezekiel 16:8, emphasis added).

The name Christians have given to the two major segments of Scripture—the Old and New *Testaments*—that is, the old and new *covenants*, reflect the truth that human salvation from sin occurs within the bonds of a covenant between God and the believer.[2] The biblical covenant is both a committed relationship between the two and an arrangement for saving the latter. The relationship is the same in the several formulations of the divine covenant (whether Abrahamic, Sinaitic/old/first, or new/second): "I . . . will be your God, and you shall be my people" (Leviticus 26:12; see also Genesis 17:2, 7-9; Jeremiah 31:33).[3]

In addition to being protective, the biblical covenant establishes *a saving relationship* between God and humanity. Within this union, divine grace operates to save and to transform the believer, bringing the human partner into harmony and oneness with God. In such a union, God totally satisfies, or, as the New Testament declares, "You are complete in Him [Christ]" (Colossians 2:10, NKJV).

Although God compares His covenant to a marriage commitment, the parallel is not exact. The marriage covenant commits two *equal* parties to a lifelong relationship. But God's covenant is established between a superior and an inferior, that is, between the divine, sinless Creator and the sinful, dependent believer. The human partner has no input into the arrangement, such as there might be in a secular contract . In the biblical arrangement, the believer can only accept or reject the covenant relationship and its provisions as God offers them.

When God organized the Israelites into a nation and entered into a solemn covenant with them at Sinai (see Exodus 19–24), they were already in a nominal union with Him by virtue of the covenant God had made earlier with their ancestor, Abraham (see Genesis 15:9-18; 17:1-27). Sinai, however, afforded an important opportunity for God to renew His covenant on a national scale with Abraham's descendants. And although some three thousand took advantage of Aaron's weak leadership at Sinai, causing the idolatrous debacle in Moses' absence (see Exodus 32:28), the people were graciously forgiven (see Exodus 33:12-17), the broken tables of the Ten Commandments were replaced (see Exodus 34:1-9), and the covenant was briefly reaffirmed with some added stipulations —and later more fully on the plains of Moab (see Exodus 34:10, 27; Deuteronomy 29:1).[4] The Sinai covenant, ratified by sacrificial blood, provided for Israel the spiritual bond with God, within which it was their privilege to live and move and have their beings (see Acts 17:28).

Since God does not change (see Malachi 3:6) and since He is the Initiator of the covenants He has made with His people, there is at the heart of Bible religion really only one covenant, the covenant of grace. The Abrahamic, Sinaitic (sometimes called "first" and "old," see Hebrews 8:13; 9:1), and the "new" ("second" by implication) covenants readily meld into one. Each succeeding covenant is simply a flowering out of the preceding arrangements.[5]

In its most complete expression, the biblical covenant, as *an arrangement* to bring about the salvation of sinners, contains three fundamental articles: (1) the covenant *promises*, affirmed by God's oath (see Galatians 3:16, 17; Ephesians 2:12; Hebrews 6:13, 17); (2) the covenant *obligations*, obedience to God's will as expressed in the moral law of the Ten Commandments (see Deuteronomy 4:13); and (3) the covenant *means* by which to meet the obligations or conditions—namely Christ, through the plan of salvation (see Isaiah 42:1, 6; Hebrews 9:1; 4:1, 2).[6]

A call to covenant loyalty

In the second precept of the Ten Commandments, God says of Himself: "I the Lord your God am a jealous God" (Exodus 20:5). To today's reader, constantly bombarded with the easy relationships of TV soap operas and Western lifestyles, the word *jealous* may seem a harsh term for God. But though Bible writers must speak to us about God in human language, divine jealousy is neither petulance nor "green-eyed" envy. When used of God, the term is more akin to zealousness—a zealousness arising from God's holy love for His people.

A proper kind of jealousy is actually the flip side of genuine love. The apostle Paul describes it as "divine jealousy" (2 Corinthians 11:2). Divine jealousy is often mentioned in the context of the covenant, recalling the relationship previously established. "Take heed to yourselves, lest you forget the covenant of the Lord your God, which he made with you, and make a graven image in the form of anything which the Lord your God has forbidden you. *For the Lord your God is a devouring fire, a jealous God*" (Deuteronomy 4:23, 24, emphasis added).

Divine jealousy not only brooks no rival, but it zealously protects its own. Idolatry displaces God from the center of the believer's life, and also leads to the abandonment of the only means available for human salvation. To break covenant with the Creator-Redeemer is to choose death, eternal death (see Deuteronomy 30:19)! A jealous God could not let His people go to ruin without attempting to win them back, even if the remedial measures seemed harsh (see Jeremiah 16:10-13).

Concerned over Judah's waywardness, Jeremiah felt constrained by God's Spirit to call the nation back to its earlier loyalty to the covenant. The providential finding of the Mosaic writings during Josiah's reign (see 2 Kings 22:8) and the renewal of the national resolve to reaffirm the covenant relationship (see 2 Kings 23:1-4) added incentive (see Jeremiah 11:1-8). The prophet was to proclaim the appeal in "the cities of Judah" as well as in Jerusalem (verse 6).

The Lord summarized for Jeremiah: "You shall say to them, Thus says the Lord, the God of Israel: Cursed be the man who does not heed the words of this covenant which I commanded your fathers when I brought them out of the land of Egypt, from the iron furnace, saying, Listen to my voice, and do all that I command you. So shall you be my people, and I will be your God, that I may perform the oath which I swore to your fathers, to give them a land flowing with milk and honey, as at this day" (verses 3-5).[7]

Momentarily thrilled by the Lord's words that seemed to imply a restored relationship with Judah, Jeremiah responded with a hearty Amen—"So be it, Lord" (verse 5).

It is psychologically sound to recall to a backslider the time when he or she experienced the joy of conversion and deliverance from the shackles of sin. So the divine message also sought to remind Judah of the marvelous deliverance their ancestors experienced from Egyptian slavery.

However, divine kindness has limits, and God firmly reminded His covenant people that obedience lay at the heart of their relationship with Him. Blessings or judgments would follow their response of covenant obedience or disobedience (see Leviticus 26; Deuteronomy 28). They could not take their relationship to Him lightly. Unfortunately, Judah turned her back on God, leaving Him no alternative but to punish His people severely with war and captivity. His jealous love would administer such discipline (see Jeremiah 11:9-12), and it would save at least a remnant of His beloved people (see Jeremiah 24:5-7).

Looking ahead

Jeremiah 30 and 31 is usually designated "the Book of Consolations," but since the topics of chapters 32 and 33 are similar, some scholars think of the four as forming a "Book of Hope."[8] At any rate, this four-chapter segment marks the climax of the prophet's theological message. Among its promises for the future Messianic age—beyond the Babylonian captivity—is the promise of a new covenant. "Behold, the days are coming, says the Lord, when I will make a new covenant with the house of Israel and the house of Judah" (see Jeremiah 31:31-34). Wedding bells would ring again, so to speak, and lasting vows would be taken.

When the provisions of the covenant are examined (see verses 31-34), however, it is striking to find little that is essentially "new" in the new covenant! The parties are the same: God and Israel/ Judah. The Ten Commandments are the same, and God has always desired to write them in the heart (see Isaiah 51:7; Psalm 37:31). The Lord would again be Israel's God, and they would be His people. Grace in the covenant for the forgiveness of sins had always been available through faith in the coming Redeemer portrayed in the rituals of the sanctuary (see Hebrews 9:1; 8:1, 2). Obviously, then, more than the sin-hardened condition of the Jews in the sixth century B.C. Judah prompted this divine promise of a new covenant.

Although the promises and obligations of the biblical covenant in its different formulations are essentially the same, that which necessitated a renewal of the covenant in the coming Messianic age was the change in the third element of the arrangement: the *means*. With the advent of the Messiah, there would be a shift from the ritual types to the antitype, to Jesus Christ Himself.

The ceremonial rituals foreshadowed the coming Redeemer and led penitent sinners to trust in Him for forgiveness of sin, but animal blood in itself could not take away sin (see Hebrews 10:4). However, with the Saviour's actual, atoning death (see Hebrews 9:26) and inauguration into His priestly ministry (see Hebrews 8:1, 2)—together with the descent of the Holy Spirit in a more extensive ministry than heretofore (see John 16:7, 8)—the renewal of the covenant became a necessity. The promised *means* became a reality in Jesus Christ by His incarnation, atoning death, resurrection, and priesthood.

The Jews forsook pagan idolatry after their long years in Babylonian exile. But on the morning of Christ's trial before Pilate, the national leadership rejected the Covenant maker Himself (see John 19:15). As a result, their national role as God's chosen agency to convey His truth to the world was transferred to the church (see

Matthew 21:43; 1 Peter 2:9, 10). The church, composed of both Jewish and Gentile believers in Christ, became the new Israel—spiritual Israel—in God's plan (see Galatians 6:15, 16) and the inheritor of the divine promises (see Galatians 3:26-29). The covenant was renewed with the church—this "remnant" of Israel (see Romans 11:5)—in the persons of Christ's disciples when He instituted the Communion supper on the eve of His death—the death that ratified the "new" covenant (see 1 Corinthians 11:25). In this manner Jesus became the Mediator of the "new" or renewed covenant foretold by Jeremiah (see Hebrews 8:6-13).

Thus, as a part of spiritual Israel, every believer in Christ enters into the new covenant relationship with God—a committed relationship, just as Israel experienced—"betrothed . . . to Christ . . . as a pure bride to her one husband" (2 Corinthians 11:2). To fraternize with the world and to adopt its philosophies and practices is to commit spiritual adultery as did ancient Israel and Judah. It is to break covenant with God. And the New Testament carries the same warning as does the Old: "You adulterous people, don't you know that friendship with the world is hatred toward God? Anyone who chooses to be a friend of the world becomes an enemy of God" (James 4:4, NIV).

Although moderns like to dabble in all religions and choose their own lifestyles—"do your own thing," as they would phrase it—the Christian faith within the bond of the new covenant is exclusive. Jesus underscored that fact Himself: "I am the way, and the truth, and the life; no one comes to the Father, *but by me*" (John 14:6, emphasis added). God is not envious in a human, selfish way of the many "so-called gods" (1 Corinthians 8:5) that seem to allure His covenant people. Rather, He is zealous to protect them from eternal loss, for the reality in our cosmos is simply this: "There is salvation in no one else [than Christ], for there is no other name under heaven given among men by which we must be saved" (Acts 4:12).

---

1. Kidner, *The Message of Jeremiah*, 33.
2. Remarks in this section on the biblical covenant are adapted from the "Adult Teaching Aids" by the author for the Adult Sabbath School Lessons: *God's Great Gift: The Everlasting Covenant* (October-December 1982), *passim*.
3. To the casual reader of the Bible, covenant terminology appears confusing because the Bible writers use different designations for the same covenant formulation. The Sinai covenant is so called because the covenant was made with Israel at

that location. It is called "first" because it was the first one made with the whole nation (see Hebrews 9:1). It is also called "old" because the sacrificial system linked with it had worn out (see Hebrews 8:13). It is also called "old" sometimes because it became perverted into a system of salvation by works (see Galatians 4:21-31). The renewal of the covenant that Jeremiah predicted is called "new" because it was reformulated later than Sinai, in the Messianic age (see Jeremiah 31:31; Hebrews 8:6-13). Jesus is the Mediator of this covenant (see Hebrews 8:6), which He ratified by His death (see Matthew 26:28; 1 Corinthians 11:25). Since the Sinai covenant is called "first," by implication, "the new covenant" would be called "second." But all formulations of the biblical covenant between God and His people (whether Abrahamic, Sinaitic, or "new") are really only formulations of God's everlasting covenant of grace.

4. See *SDABC*, 1:671, 675, 1058.

5. *ISBE*, 1:792; George A. F. Knight, *Theology as Narration* (Grand Rapids, Mich.: William B. Eerdmans Publishing Co., 1976), 130, 131.

6. In Old Testament times, the gospel and plan of salvation were taught by means of the sacrificial system. Through symbol and rite, the patriarchs and Israel learned to exercise faith in the coming Redeemer. In this manner the penitent could find forgiveness for sin and release from guilt. The blessings of the covenant could thus be retained, and spiritual growth—restoring the image of God in the life—could continue on. The same forgiveness and renewal is found by the believer in Christ today under the provisions of the new covenant and Christ's priestly ministry in the heavenly sanctuary.

7. Ellen White's comment on the covenant made at Sinai underscores the validity of the renewal of the biblical covenant at that time: "The covenant that God made with His people at Sinai is to be our refuge and defense. . . . This covenant is of just as much force today as it was when the Lord made it with ancient Israel" (Ellen G. White Comments, *SDABC*, 1:1103).

8. Kidner, *The Message of Jeremiah*, 102, 112. Note titles.

Chapter 5

The Praying Prophet

John Welch, a minister of the gospel, felt so great a burden for souls that he often rose in the night to plead with God for their salvation. On one occasion his wife begged with him to regard his health. His answer was, "O woman, I have the souls of three thousand to answer for, and I know not how it is with them."[1]

Pastor Welch and the prophet Jeremiah had at least one thing in common: both were great intercessors; prayer was the breath of their souls. In the picturesque phrase of an old Lancashire woman, both were "very thick with the Almighty."[2] Although living in different dispensations, both knelt, as it were, in the "knee prints" of humanity's greatest intercessor, Jesus Christ Himself, who often prayed in the hours before the dawn (see Mark 1:35), and at times even through the night (see Luke 6:12).

Jeremiah is characterized as the "weeping prophet," but he equally deserves the title of the "praying prophet." At least a dozen of his prayers are recorded—the shortest being but a single sentence in English (see Jeremiah 4:10), the longest, nine verses (see Jeremiah 32:17-25). No other Bible personality has left in the inspired record as many prayers as this prophet who walked and talked with God throughout his forty-plus years of ministry.

Any reader of the prayers is struck by Jeremiah's "spirit of holy familiarity."[3] They are respectful, but not in a formal, carefully phrased way. Rather, they are marked by vigorous conversation and challenging questions. The second characteristic is Jeremiah's openness. Nothing is hidden or held back. He is completely candid, and his pain and frustrations are poured into the Lord's listening ear. Sometimes God responds immediately; sometimes He meets the prophet's cry with silence, letting His emotionally drained messenger recover himself.

It is only natural to wonder how Jeremiah's personal talks with God came to be recorded in the book that bears his name. It is doubtful that Baruch (his secretary) was privy to the prophet's prayer life. It may be suggested that these are "diary" prayers, that the prophet himself composed them, writing as he "talked" with God and waited for His answers.

As the arrangement of the book now stands, the bulk of the prayers are found in chapters 12 to 20, for which reason this segment is sometimes labeled "The Confessions of Jeremiah" or the "The Laments of Jeremiah." A few of these prayers we noted earlier in chapter 2. We turn now to examine other petitions.

Prayer of protest (Jeremiah 4:10)

"Ah, Lord God, surely thou hast utterly deceived this people and Jerusalem, saying, 'It shall be well with you'; whereas the sword has reached their very life ["is at our throats," NIV]" (Jeremiah 4:10).

Is Jeremiah blaming God for the people's confusion? This much-debated prayer is probably best understood in the light of the Hebrew thought pattern that often omits second causes and views God as the First Cause of every happening. Thus, God is often said to do things that we (in Western lands) would say He permits, or doesn't prevent.[4]

The context indicates that Jeremiah had just announced the coming invasions of the Babylonians (see Jeremiah 4:5-8). As a result, the courage of the Jewish court would fail, the priests would be appalled, and the prophets would be "astounded" (verse 9). But why would the prophets be astonished? What did they teach? On another occasion Jeremiah answered that question himself: "The prophets say to them, 'You shall not see the sword, nor shall you have famine, *but I will give you assured peace in this place*' " (Jeremiah 14:13, emphasis added, see also chapters 6:13, 14; 8:11).

The *false prophets*, not God, were promising the nation peace. In contrast, Jeremiah announced destruction by the Babylonian sword. Young Jeremiah sensed the confusion of the people. It seemed to him that God was sending (permitting) a double message of peace and sword, and he protested this condition of things. Why did God permit the false prophets to speak in His name? From the people's point of view, it would seem that the class of persons called "prophets" (which would include Jeremiah) were announcing two diametrically opposed messages. Thus, it would seem that God was sending mixed signals and permitting the people to be deceived.

But the Lord made no reply to His frustrated servant. Truth always has its counterfeit, but they can be distinguished. As Jesus was to affirm many centuries later: "If any man's will is to do his [God's] will, he shall know whether the teaching is from God or whether I am speaking on my own authority" (John 7:17).

The nation now had no excuse for lacking knowledge of the divine will after the high priest Hilkiah had recovered the sacred Scriptures. God urged them in figurative language: "Stand by the roads, and look, and ask for the ancient paths, where the good way is; and walk in it, and find rest for your souls" (Jeremiah 6:16). A simple testing of Jeremiah's message and that of the other, so-called prophets by the writings of Moses would have determined who spoke the truth.

Prayer of partiality (Jeremiah 10:23-25)

Jeremiah's prayers reflect his spiritual growth. This may be discerned even in his intercessory prayers. His earliest recorded intercession (see Jeremiah 10:23-25) was prompted by God's statement that He would deport the nation from their homeland. "Behold, I am slinging out the inhabitants of the land at this time, and I will bring distress on them, that they may feel it" (Jeremiah 10:18). The prophet also sensed the impact of the predicted invasion: "Hark, a rumor! Behold, it comes!—a great commotion out of the north country to make the cities of Judah a desolation, a lair of jackals" (verse 22).

In response to this frightening announcement of the divine purpose, Jeremiah intercedes for Judah. His prayer contains three petitions: (1) "I know, O Lord, that the way of man is not in himself, that it is not in man who walks to direct his steps" (verse 23); (2) "correct me, O Lord, but in just measure; not in thy anger, lest thou bring me to nothing" (verse 24); (3) "pour out thy wrath upon the nations that know thee not, . . . for they have devoured Jacob . . . and have laid waste his habitation" (verse 25).

In the first petition (verse 23), Jeremiah seems to state a universal truth. But in the context of this chapter, the prophet is excusing Judah's sinful condition. Jeremiah was presenting their case something like this: "Lord, You are about to punish Your people with a terrible destruction. True, they have sinned against You. But

You know, Lord, that it's not possible for anyone to live right on his own. Judah has drifted from You and has stumbled as a consequence. The people need discipline, but correct them only 'in measure' [I speak as their representative], but not in great anger, lest You annihilate the nation. If wrath must be poured out, pour it out on Judah's enemies. They don't acknowledge Your authority, and they are destroying Your people."

Again, the Lord remains silent to His servant's petition. In time, Jeremiah would realize the truly sin-hardened condition of the nation and the necessity for the severe judgment. Years later—when the prophet had come to see matters as God saw them—the Lord said through him: "Fear not, O Jacob my servant, says the Lord, for I am with you. I will make a full end of all the nations to which I have driven you, but of you I will not make a full end. I will chasten you in just measure, and I will by no means leave you unpunished" (Jeremiah 46:28). Jeremiah's prayer of many years before—prayed in ignorant sincerity—eventually was answered in the manner God saw would be best.

Prayer of intercession (Jeremiah 14:7–15:4)

Jeremiah's most extensive intercession crosses two chapters in our modern Bibles (14:7–15:4). The prophet presents three pleas (see Jeremiah 14:7-9, 13, 19-22), and three times the Lord responds (see Jeremiah 14:10-12, 17, 18; 15:1-4).

A severe drought prompted Jeremiah's prayer (see Jeremiah 14:1-6). The prophet doubtlessly recognized the natural disaster as one of the curses/judgments due to the national violation of the covenant (see Deuteronomy 28:15, 23, 24). Because the people were indifferent in their suffering, he would plead for them and confess their sins: "Though our iniquities testify against us, *act, O Lord for thy name's sake*; for our backslidings are many, we have sinned against thee" (Jeremiah 14:7, emphasis added).

In spite of our sins, Lord, act—send rain, and deliver us from foreign destruction *for the honor of Your name*. This is the argument Moses used on more than one occasion to avert God's righteous judgment on rebellious Israel (see Exodus 32:10-12; Numbers 14:12-20). Recalling Israel's history in Egypt and the Exodus, God pointed out to Ezekiel that on three different occasions "I acted *for the sake of my name*, that it should not be profaned in the sight of the nations, in whose sight I had brought them out" (Ezekiel 20:14, emphasis added; see also verses 9, 22). Jeremiah now switches to another line of reasoning:

O thou hope of Israel, its savior in time of trouble, why shouldst thou be like a stranger . . . , like a wayfarer who [tarries] for a night? Why shouldst thou be like a man confused, like a mighty man who cannot save? (Jeremiah 14:8, 9).

Jeremiah is the only Bible writer to employ the epithet "Hope of Israel" as God's name (see Jeremiah 17:13), although the concept is expressed elsewhere. Truly, God was Judah's only hope, but Judah was not interested in assistance from that quarter. Nevertheless, Jeremiah began to challenge what seemed to him to be God's indifference by comparing Him to a tourist passing through Judah's cities and countryside to see the sights, but oblivious to the national needs (see Jeremiah 14:8). He next compared God to a confused person, not sure what he ought to do (verse 9). And finally, the prophet likens God to a warrior who, in spite of his reputed strength, has in some manner been rendered helpless (verse 9).

Probably realizing that he had been treading close to blasphemy, the prophet moved to more solid ground: "You are in our midst; we are Your children—we bear Your name and belong to You. Don't abandon Your own!" (see verse 9).

The Lord responds immediately and decisively: "As far as Judah is concerned, 'They have loved to wander thus, they have not restrained their feet.' Consequently, I do not accept them and will punish them for their sins. Furthermore, 'Do not pray for the welfare of this people.' Though they fast and sacrifice, 'I will not accept them; but I will consume them by the sword, by famine, and by pestilence' " (verses 10-12). This was the third time the Lord commanded the prophet to desist from interceding for Judah (see Jeremiah 7:16; 11:14).

Upon hearing God's refusal to save Judah from certain ruin, Jeremiah attempted another approach. Perhaps, if God realized that the people were being influenced by the false prophets, He would be less severe with them. "Ah, Lord God, behold, the prophets say to them, 'You shall not see the sword, nor shall you have famine, but I will give you assured peace in this place' " (Jeremiah 14:13).

But, the Lord explained, He had never sent these men or ordered them to speak in His name. "They are prophesying to you a lying vision, worthless divination, and the deceit of their own minds" (verse 14). Both the false prophets and their deluded victims would perish.

As Jeremiah sensed the doom that was determined, the pressure of his emotions built up to the point that at first he seemed to lash out at God. "Hast thou utterly rejected Judah?" he cried. "Does thy soul loathe Zion?" Foolishly, the prophet demands, "Why hast thou smitten us so that there is no healing for us? We looked for peace, but no good came; for a time of healing, but behold, terror." Momentarily, Jeremiah fell into the rut of blaming God for the national disquiet!

As his fervor cooled a little, the prophet admitted that the real problem was Judah's gross apostasy, and he exclaimed: "We acknowledge our wickedness, O Lord, and the iniquity of our fathers, for we have sinned against thee" (verse 20). He seems to be saying, "What more can we do?" But Jeremiah, the patriot-prophet was out of time with the temper of his people. As God's loyal flag bearer, he was far out in front of the troops; they were not following his signal or responding to his urgent cries. Judah was marching in another direction, under the order of another leader!

But the prophet made one more earnest, impassioned plea: "Do not spurn us, for thy name's sake [for the honor of Your name among the nations]; do not dishonor thy glorious throne [by permitting the demolition of the temple, where, in the Shekinah glory, You sit "enthroned upon the cherubim" (Psalm 99:1; see also Leviticus 16:2)]; remember and do not break thy covenant with us [see Leviticus 26:9-12]." You are the Creator, who can control the rains. "We set our hope on thee" (verses 21, 22).

The Lord's third response was summary and immediately terminated Jeremiah's intercession. "The Lord said to me, 'Though Moses and Samuel stood before me [two of Israel's greatest intercessors], yet my heart would not turn toward this people. Send them out of my sight, and let them go!' " (Jeremiah 15:1). Only the reaping of sin's bitter harvest would make possible the salvation of a remnant (see verses 2-4).

We moderns must not misjudge Jeremiah. He "was a man of like nature with ourselves" (see James 5:17). God did not reprove him for his foolish outbursts. He perceived the prophet's generous, sympathetic heart that longed to save his people and to see them fulfilling God's ideal. The Lord ached for their salvation even more.

As any parent knows, kindness and mercy have their limits, and strong disciplinary action is then the only thing that can right a situation. God graciously let Jeremiah spill out his frustrations and charges; then kindly—but firmly—He corrected the prophet's faulty thinking.

Prayer for grace (Jeremiah 17:13–18)

We move now to a quiet conversation in which Jeremiah talks over Judah's situation and prays for saving grace himself (see Jeremiah 17:13-18). Again, he addresses God by the title of his own coining: "O Lord, the hope of Israel, all who forsake thee shall be put to shame; those who turn away from thee shall be written in the earth, for they have forsaken the Lord, the fountain of living water" (verse 13).

To abandon God is to commit spiritual suicide. Hear the death sentence on the human race echoing through the prophet's factual statement: "You are dust, and to dust you shall return" (Genesis 3:19). The phrase "written in the earth" probably alludes to the ultimate destruction of the lost (see Proverbs 11:31).

Others might forsake the Hope of Israel, but not Jeremiah. He confidently pleaded for himself: "Heal me, O Lord, and I shall be healed; save me, and I shall be saved; for thou art my praise." The Hebrew word translated "heal" in this instance can be used to describe either physical or spiritual healing (see Numbers 12:13; Isaiah 6:10). But it is also evident from the parallelism in the petition that "heal me" means the same as "save me" (Jeremiah 17:14).

The revelation of God that Jeremiah sought to portray to his countrymen, he had himself perceived. The carrier of living water to the people had himself drunk of the same (see Jeremiah 2:13; 17:13). The arrows of grace had pierced the prophet's own heart, and he had turned to the Balm of Gilead for healing (see Jeremiah 8:22). If Jeremiah saved no other, his work was not in vain, for he found salvation himself!

Next, in his prayer, the prophet moved back to the people—to the hard core who had defiantly challenged him: " 'Where is the word of the Lord? Let it come!' They taunt me, Lord, because the predicted ruin hasn't come. But You know I haven't urged You to hasten our national destruction. Instead, I have urged You to withhold it. What I proclaimed to the leaders and people, I received from You" (see Jeremiah 17:15, 16).

The final petition (verses 17, 18) is thought by some to be vindictive: "Don't be a terror to me, but be my refuge when the war comes. 'Let those be put to shame who persecute me, but let me not be put to shame.' "

However, the petition appears more like an appeal to God's original promise. God said then, "Do not be dismayed by them. . . . I make you this day a fortified city, an iron pillar, and bronze walls. . . for I am with you, says the Lord, to deliver you" (Jeremiah 1:17-19).

"Please, Lord," Jeremiah seems to be saying, "in the final crash, honor Your promises to me. Vindicate me and Your message by letting the judgment fall where it ought to fall 'with double destruction' "—the Hebrew way of saying "ample" or "complete" punishment (see Jeremiah 16:18; Isaiah 40:2).

A prayer of astonishment (Jeremiah 32:16-25)

True to God's word, the Babylonian forces attacked Jerusalem and laid siege to the capital for thirty months (see Jeremiah 52: 4-6). During a lull, when the siege was briefly lifted, Jeremiah started home to Anathoth. A sentry recognized him as he walked through the Gate of Benjamin and denounced him as a deserter. The protesting prophet was arrested and imprisoned. He remained incarcerated until released by the Babylonians at the end of the war (see Jeremiah 37:12-15, 21; 38:28).

At the height of the siege (see Jeremiah 32:1, 2), God revealed to Jeremiah that his cousin Hanamel was coming to request the prophet to buy a tract of land from him in Anathoth, since Jeremiah had the kinship right to purchase it (see Leviticus 25:25-28). The cousin came as God had said (see Jeremiah 32:7, 8).

Apparently Jeremiah surmised the divine purpose and made the transaction as public as possible. The silver was weighed out, the deeds—written in duplicate—were signed, and the prisoners and guards in the court of the prison functioned as witnesses. Jeremiah charged Baruch to place the sealed and open deeds in a clay jar for preservation "that they may last for a long time." Then under the prophetic impulse of the Spirit, he announced: "For thus says the Lord of hosts, the God of Israel: Houses and fields and vineyards shall again be bought in this land" (verses 14, 15).

After Hanamel and Baruch had left, one with silver and the other with the evidence of sale, the astonished Jeremiah, perhaps withdrawing to his small sleeping area, began to talk with God about the remarkable transaction. As he talked, he probably could hear the cries of the troops in battle on the walls and the thud of the Babylonian battering rams striking against the top levels with a steady regularity.

"Ah Lord God!" he prayed. "It is thou who hast made the heavens and the earth by thy great power and by thy outstretched arm! Nothing is too hard for thee." This vital truth, learned at his mother's knee and often repeated, had apparently come to be a kind of cliché repeated without thought—as the end of his prayer shows. In true Jewish manner, the prophet continued by listing God's attributes and powers and His deliverance of Israel from Egypt and His placement of them in Palestine (see verses 18-24).

Then the amazed prophet switched to the ongoing war. It had taken place as God had foretold. "The siege mounds have come up to the city"; the sword, famine, and pestilence ravaged the city's defenders and citizens. "Yet thou, O Lord God, hast said to me, 'Buy the field for money and get witnesses'—though the city is given into the hands of the Chaldeans" (verses 24, 25).

Jeremiah broke off from talking with the Lord. The whole transaction was too incredible, and he lapsed into silence. Even at the moment he gave Hanamel the silver, the very property itself was in Babylonian hands! For practical purposes, the country was conquered. It would be only a matter of time, and Jerusalem's defenses would crumble. Zedekiah's rebellion would be met with harsh reprisals. The national collapse was not only imminent and certain, but probably permanent! Already Jeremiah had forgotten his assertion: "Nothing is too hard for Thee"!

But the Lord responded to His wondering servant by restating those very same words in the form of a question: "Behold, I am the Lord, the God of all flesh; *is anything too hard for me?*" (verse 27, emphasis added). After reiterating His purpose to discipline His people by conquest and captivity (verses 28-36), the Lord repeated His promise to restore them (verses 37-40). "I will rejoice in doing them good, and I will plant them in this land in faithfulness, *with all my heart and all my soul*" (verse 41, emphasis added). "Fields shall be bought for money, and deeds shall be signed and sealed and witnessed, in the land of Benjamin" (verse 44). The transaction demanded a stout faith, but the promise was as sure as God Himself.

When we review and analyze the prayers of Jeremiah, it is fully evident that open, uninhibited conversation with God was a natural way of life with him. He was a bold intercessor. There is not much praise in the prophet's petitions, but God never repelled His servant's attempts to "reason together" with Him (see Isaiah 1:18).

---

1. Cited by Ellen G. White, *Gospel Workers* (Washington, D.C.: Review and Herald Publishing Association, 1915), 31.

2. Ibid., 255.

3. Charles L. Feinberg, *Jeremiah*, vol. 6 of *The Expositor's Bible Commentary* (Grand Rapids, Mich.: Zondervan Publishing House, 1986), 457. Hereafter cited as *ExpoBC*.

4. For example, God is said to harden Pharaoh (see Exodus 9:12), to send Joseph into slavery (see Genesis 45:5, 8), to send the Assyrians against Israel (see Isaiah 10:5, 6), to send strong delusions on unbelievers (see 2 Thessalonians 2:11), etc.

Chapter 6
God's Object Lessons

Jesus Christ was the Master Teacher. He commonly linked abstract truth with familiar objects so that His hearers might easily understand Him. The natural world and the activities of daily life provided visual aids that still repeat His lessons.

> The birds of the air, the lilies of the field, the sower and the seed, the shepherd and the sheep—with these Christ illustrated immortal truth. He drew illustrations also from the events of life, facts of experience familiar to the hearers—the leaven, the hid treasure, the pearl, the fishing net, the lost coin, the prodigal son, the houses on the rock and the sand. In His lessons there was something to interest every mind, to appeal to every heart.[1]

Jesus adapted the practice of the Hebrew prophets, especially Jeremiah and Ezekiel. These two men often illustrated their prophetic proclamations with visual aids—such as Ezekiel's striking "sandbox" model of Jerusalem under siege (see Ezekiel 4, 5), or Jeremiah's shattering a clay flask in the Valley of Hinnom before a select party of leaders (see Jeremiah 19:1, 10). We may correctly say that it was "the Spirit of Christ within them" (1 Peter 1:11) who directed these prophets to select their visual aids!

The Lord sought every possible avenue to communicate His messages to Judah. The visual aids encapsulated in Jeremiah's writings still impart forceful messages to modern Christians because human nature doesn't change from one era to the next. In this chapter we will explore several of these visual aids—some were word figures; others were concrete visible objects.

Of men and birds (Jeremiah 8:4-7)

The Lord gave a double-featured illustration to Jeremiah to proclaim in the opening years of his ministry (see Jeremiah 8:4-7). This short passage hangs on the Hebrew word *shûb* (turn "back; return"), which is used explicitly six times and implied a couple more times. As can be seen from its English equivalents, *shûb* can carry either the nuance "to turn back" (apostatize) or "to return" (convert).

The Lord spoke through Jeremiah from the perspective that Judah had broken covenant with Him and had turned away: "When men fall, do they not rise again?" Here the idea of *shûb* is implied. Common sense tells us that a person who stumbles and falls attempts to *return* to an erect position! Again, God asked: "If one *turns away* [*shûb*], does he not return [*shûb*]?" When a traveler discovers that he is on the wrong road, he hurriedly retraces his route, even if it is necessary to travel a score of miles or more to where he took the wrong turn.

Then God applied these figures: "Why then has this people *turned away* [*shûb*] in perpetual *backsliding* [*shûb* root]? They hold fast to deceit, they refuse *to return* [*shûb*]. . . . No man repents of his wickedness, saying, 'What have I done?' Every one *turns* [*shûb*] to his own course, like a horse plunging headlong into battle" (verses 5, 6). Once the Mosiac writings had been found and made public, the national leader knew the nation was on the wrong road and headed for disaster. Common sense dictated a genuine return to the old ways (see Jeremiah 3:10; 6:16).

But perhaps the citizens of Judah were too close to their situation to reason aright, so God called their attention to the remarkable migratory habits of certain birds. "Even the stork in the heavens knows her times; and the turtledove, swallow, and crane keep the time of their coming; but my people know not the ordinance of the Lord" (verse 7).

The migratory birds leave their winter quarters for the nesting areas, but, true to their instincts, they *return*. Theirs is an instinctive fidelity to the laws imprinted by the Creator on their genetic makeup. Although human obedience to moral law is not instinctive and requires the exercise of choice, yet Judah's conscience had been educated in years past by the Ten Commandments. It had been God's design (within the covenant relationship) to "write" these principles of His will in their minds (see Deuteronomy 6:6; Psalm 40:8; Isaiah 51:7).

Judah's "spiritual" instincts should have aroused her to get up from her fall (apostasy) and to get back on the right road again. But, alas, the national conscience was "seared" (see 1 Timothy 4:2). Ironically, since the Fall, nature is more faithful to the will of the Creator than is humanity, who was appointed nature's ruler (see Genesis 1:26, 28)!

Rechabite refugees (Jeremiah 35)

King Jehoiakim's revolt against his overlord Nebuchadnezzar resulted in the savaging of the land by guerrilla bands (see 2 Kings 24:1, 2). Among those who fled this new danger were the nomadic families of the Rechabites. These crowded into Jerusalem, along with other refugees, seeking the protection of its walls.

Although the Rechabites worshiped Yahweh and had distant blood ties with the Jews, they remained distinct from the Israelites and never were absorbed. Their genealogical line extended back to Abraham, whose son Midian (by his wife Keturah), fathered the tribe of the Midianites (see Genesis 25:1-4). Some family (or families) of the Midianites intermarried with the Kenites, a tribe that lived in Canaan long before Abraham's pilgrimage there (see Genesis 15:19). Jethro, Moses' father-in-law, descended from that mixed group, inasmuch as he is called a Kenite as well as a Midianite (see Judges 1:16; Numbers 10:29). Because his in-laws knew the Sinai wilderness well, Moses invited his brother-in-law Hobab to accompany Israel on their trek to Canaan to function "as eyes for us" (see Numbers 10:29-32). Several Kenite families joined the Israelite migration and eventually settled in Canaan with the tribe of Judah (see Judges 1:16).

It is from these Kenites that Rechab—and his more famous ancestor, Jehonadab (shortened to Jonadab)—descended (1 Chronicles 2:55). Jonadab—the hero of Jeremiah's enacted parable—appears on the biblical scene as a close friend of Jehu and a participant in that king's massacre of the Baal devotees at the idol's temple in Samaria (see 2 Kings 10:15-28).

Heads turned and many eyes watched as Jeremiah assembled the leaders of the Rechabites and their families in the court of the temple, dressed in their Bedouin attire. They were directed to enter one of the side chambers, where cups and pitchers of wine were placed before them. They looked in surprise and wonderment at the wine and then at Jeremiah, their host, as he invited them to refresh themselves: "Drink wine" (see Jeremiah 35:1-5).

Perhaps curious Jews, looking through the open door, heard the straightforward response of Jaazaniah, the clan leader: "We will drink no wine, for Jonadab the son of Rechab, our father [ancestor], commanded us, 'You shall not drink wine, neither you nor your sons for ever; you shall not build a house; you shall not sow seed; you shall not plant or have a vineyard; but you shall live in tents all your days, that you may live many days in the land where you sojourn.' We have obeyed the voice of Jonadab the son of Rechab, our father" (verses 6-8).

Then Jaazaniah explained what appeared to be a compromise: their presence in Jerusalem. The unsettled conditions of war made the countryside unsafe. They momentarily were in Jerusalem for the safety of their wives and children (see verse 11).

No explanation is given for Jonadab's charge. He evidently saw the evils of alcoholic drinking compounded by the problems of city life. But the amazing fact was that after approximately 240 years, his descendants were still obedient to his commandment!

Jeremiah was then directed by the Lord to publicize this episode in the temple and to point out the intended contrast: "The sons of Jonadab the son of Rechab have kept the command which their father gave them, but this people has not obeyed me" (verse 16).

Rechabite faithfulness for over two centuries is a sobering visual aid to any generation. The tribe obeyed to the letter the charge of a relative—a human being; by contrast, Judah flaunted the expressed commands of the Deity—the Creator (see verse 14). Jonadab probably gave his charge only once, presumably on his deathbed, but God had been sending His prophets "persistently" for many years to an indifferent Judah (see verse 15). These concerns of Jonadab were meant for the well-being of his people in this life, but God's concerns for Judah involved their eternal interests as well.[2] The prestige of Jeremiah as God's prophet, the location of the test—Yahweh's temple—and the fact that the clan had already compromised Jonadab's charge by moving into Jerusalem combined to exert enormous pressures on the Rechabites to yield just this once and drink the wine.[3] But the Rechabites exhibited a hearty fidelity to their ancestor's charge and passed the test with flying colors!

Shattered flask (Jeremiah 19)

Little did Jeremiah realize how expensive would be his purchase of a clay *baqbuq* for a visual aid. The *baqbuq* was a decanter with a narrow neck that aerated the water when it was poured.[4] That day, the reaction to his proclamations was swift and violent: a flogging and a night of torture in the temple stocks (see Jeremiah 19:1; 20:1, 2; Deuteronomy 25:3).

The Lord commanded the prophet to take a few elders and "senior priests" through the Potsherd Gate into the infamous "valley of the son of Hinnom" on the south side of Jerusalem. He was to take the *baqbuq* with him. (As found in archaeological excavations, these flasks range from four to ten inches in height.)

Although previously desecrated by Josiah (see 2 Kings 23:10), during the reigns of Jehoiakim and Zedekiah, the valley served once again as an active center for the most repugnant rites. While priests and elders watched, parents—assisted by priests of Baal and Molech—sacrificed and burned their innocent children upon the altars and prostrated themselves before the idols.

The pungent odor of burning incense filled the air, and the watchers could not escape the stench of burning human flesh. Above the chants of the cultic priests and the noise of clanging cymbals, Jeremiah expressed the dismay and judgment of God. Gesturing toward the scene with the flask, he cried:

"Hear the word of the Lord. . . . I am bringing such evil upon this place that the ears of every one who hears of it will tingle . . . , because they have filled this place with the blood of innocents . . . to burn their sons in the fire as burnt offerings . . . which I did not command or decree, nor did it come into my mind" (Jeremiah 19:3-5). The day is approaching, declared the prophet, when this valley will no more be referred to as Topheth, or the valley of Hinnom. It will be called the "valley of Slaughter" (verse 6).

As Jeremiah began to describe the curses/judgments of the broken covenant, he poured the flask water upon the ground.[5] The verbalized judgments poured down upon the prophet's hearers: mass slaughter of the people by a savage soldiery who would leave the bodies for the birds and beasts to devour. Now, without qualms, the people sacrificed their children to idols, but in the coming siege, they would "eat the flesh of their sons and their daughters, and...neighbor" (verse 9; see also Leviticus 26:29, 30; Deuteronomy 28:49-57).

As the elders and priests listened with growing consternation, Jeremiah hurled the flask to the ground, smashing it to pieces. "So will I break this people and this city," cried the prophet, "as one breaks a potter's vessel, so that it can never be mended. Men shall bury in Topheth because there will be no place else to bury" (verse 11).[6]

That evening Jeremiah was arrested.

Linen waistcloth (Jeremiah 13:1-11)

The covenant bond meant that Judah was "special" to God. This is underscored several times in the writings of Moses. At Sinai the Lord promised: "If you will obey my voice and keep my covenant, you shall be *my own possession* ["a peculiar treasure unto me," KJV]" (Exodus 19:5). On the plains of Moab, Moses assured the nation once more of the Lord's delight in them: "You are a people holy to the Lord your God; the Lord your God has chosen you to be *a people for his own possession* . . . because the Lord loves you, and is keeping the oath which he swore to your fathers" (Deuteronomy 7:6-8, emphasis added).[7]

God's regard for Israel and Judah as His "own possession" is graphically illustrated by the enacted parable of the linen waistcloth. The Lord instructed Jeremiah: "Go and buy a linen waistcloth, and put it on." The prophet did so (Jeremiah 13:1, 2).

The NIV translators render the Hebrew 'ēzôr as "belt," but more likely it designates the short, wrapped skirt (thigh-length) that we see worn by men who are depicted on the Egyptian and Assyrian monuments.[8] We do not know how long the prophet wore this basic undergarment, probably not long, since he was not to wash it (verse 1). But at some point he is ordered to take the garment "to the Euphrates" and to hide it "in a cleft of the rock" (verse 4).

The parable may carry a double thrust: (1) In the coming Babylonian captivity, God would mar, would humble, the great pride of His people, even though they were His most precious possession (verse 9). (2) More subtly: Judah—going after other gods, such as the gods of Assyria and Babylon, according to Ezekiel (see Ezekiel 16:28, 29; 23:1-18)—had already marred herself like the waistcloth and was now good for nothing in God's sight.

The Lord explained to Jeremiah His original intention for the combined Jewish nations—as signified by this close-fitting garment: "As the waistcloth clings to the loins of a man, so I made the whole house of Israel and the whole house of Judah cling to me . . . but they would not listen" (see Jeremiah 13:11).

God's purpose for His people is borne out by the literary arrangement of the passage, a chiastic scheme. The three commands (verses 1-7) seem to be balanced in reverse order by the three-part interpretation (verses 8-11).[9] The passage may be diagrammed in brief as follows:

A. Prophet purchases and wears a waistcloth (verses 1, 2).
　　B. Prophet removes and hides waistcloth (verses 3-5).
　　　　C. Prophet finds waistcloth useless (verses 6, 7).
　　　　C' God will render Judah useless (verses 8, 9).
　　B' Judah removes herself from God (verse 10).
A' God intended "to wear" His people like a waistcloth (verse 11).

On the negative side, it is easy to see from this literary arrangement that C and C' come at the center of the chiasm and emphasize the coming judgment that would mar and render the nation of Judah "good for nothing." But it is also evident that A and A' highlight what had been God's fond hope for His own dear possession.

God had desired that the bond between Israel/Judah and Himself would have been as close as a man's undergarment is to his body. And that He might have proudly worn them, as it were, for "a praise, and a glory" (verse 11). That is, God had hoped that the union would have been so intimate that it could have been said of them, as Jesus later said of Himself, "If you have seen My people Israel, you have seen Me. Their character is just like Mine" (see John 14:9).

Wooden yokes (Jeremiah 27)

The enacted parable of the ox yoke occurred in Zedekiah's fourth year (594/593 B.C.). It was a political parable, played out against a background of intrigue and plots of revolt.

According to the Babylonian Chronicle, a rebellion erupted in the province of Babylonia against Nebuchadnezzar's rule that took the king two months to suppress (December 595-January 594 B.C.). "In the tenth year the king of Akkad [Nebuchadnezzar] (was) in his own land; from the month of Kislev to the month of Tebet there was rebellion in Akkad. . . . With arms he slew many of his own army. His own hand captured his enemy."[10]

Zedekiah's fourth year began in the fall of 594 B.C., less than a year after Nebuchadnezzar put down the revolt in the eastern part of his empire. In that same regnal year, the Jewish king made the long trip to Babylon (see Jeremiah 51:59). The short time elapsed between the rebellion and its suppression in the east and Zedekiah's trip to Babylon from the west suggests that Nebuchadnezzar was attempting to secure Zedekiah's loyalty to the crown (and probably the loyalty of other rulers in the west, as well).

The extrabiblical evidence now available suggests that the erection of the golden image on the Plain of Dura and the assembling of the nation's officialdom to its worship was (at the heart of it) an attempt by Nebuchadnezzar to extract a loyalty oath to himself and empire from his subordinates in administration. There is little doubt that the worship of the image was tied in some manner to the worship of the national state and its interests.

The event took place sometime in 594/593 B.C., although it is possible that various groupings of officials came at different times to participate in the ritual. At some point in that year, it is quite probable that Zedekiah hypocritically rendered his obeisance to Nebuchadnezzar before the golden image. The events of chapter 27 are thought to have taken place in the late spring of 593 B.C., after the western vassal kings returned from Babylon.[11]

"Make yourself thongs and yoke-bars, and put them on your neck," God commanded the prophet. "Send word to the . . . envoys who have come to Jerusalem to Zedekiah king of Judah" (Jeremiah 27:2, 3). The envoys alluded to were from five political areas and had assembled at the court of Judah, evidently to discuss the possibility of a mass revolt in the *west* against Babylon. The *eastern* uprising was fresh in their minds; the duplicity of Zedekiah and the other kings is in character.

Into this assembly of plotters the prophet strode, bearing the model of a cattle yoke on his neck (the Hebrew text indicates that he made a model yoke for each of the ambassadors as well). " 'Thus says the Lord of hosts, the God of Israel,' " Jeremiah announced to his startled listeners. "I am the Creator of the earth and its inhabitants. 'Now I have given all these lands into the hand of Nebuchadnezzar, the king of Babylon, my servant. . . . If any nation or kingdom will not serve this Nebuchadnezzar . . . , and put its neck under the yoke of the king of Babylon, I will punish that nation with the sword, with famine, and with pestilence. . . . But any nation which will bring its neck under the yoke of the king of Babylon and serve him, I will leave on its own land, to till it and dwell there, says the Lord' " (verses 4-11).

The yoke dangling around the prophet's neck not only spoke of submission, but it also pointed to Heaven's sovereignty. God rules in the kingdoms of men (see Daniel 4:17, 25, 32; John 19:11). Unwittingly, the Nebuchadnezzars and Cyruses are His "servants"/"shepherds," doing His bidding (see Jeremiah 27:6; Isaiah 44:28) as He works out His eternal purpose in the earth.

---

1. Ellen G. White, *Education* (Boise, Idaho: Pacific Press Publishing Association, 1952), 102.

2. Feinberg, *Jeremiah*, in *ExpoBC*, 6:602.

3. Kidner, *The Message of Jeremiah*, 118.

4. *ISBE*, 2:967, 968.

5. The expression "I will make *void*" (Jeremiah 19:7, RSV, KJV) is translated from the Hebrew verb *baqaq*, which means "to empty." The Hebrew name of the flask Jeremiah purchased (*baquq*) is derived from this verb. Thus God literally said, "I will empty or pour out the plans of Judah." The use of this verb implies that the prophet actually poured water from the flask as he spoke.

6. The "valley of the son of Hinnom"—shortened to the "valley of Hinnom" (Hebrew: *ge hinnom*) was transliterated as *geenna* (English: *Gehenna*) into the Greek New Testament, where it appears twelve times and is translated "hell" (KJV). Because, by means of the Babylonian war, it became known as the "valley of Slaughter"—a place of God's judgment (see Jeremiah 7:32, 19:6, 7), it is easy to see how the valley came to symbolize the final destruction of the wicked in the New Testament (see Matthew 5:22, 29, 30; 10:28; 18:9; 23:15, 33; Mark 9:43, 45, 47; Luke 12:5; James 3:6).

7. See also Deuteronomy 14:2; 26:18; Psalm 135:4; Malachi 3:17. The New Testament carries a similar thought for the new Israel, the church (see Titus 2:14; 1 Peter 2:9).

8. *ANEP*, Figs. 1, 2, 8, 1, 4.

9. See Brueggemann, *To Pluck Up, to Tear Down*, 121, 122.

10. See William H. Shea, "Daniel 3: Extra-Biblical Texts and the Convocation on the Plain of Dura," *Andrews University Seminary Studies* 20 (Spring 1982): 29-52, for a suggested reconstruction of the historical background.

11. Ibid., 51.

Chapter 7

A New Start

No attribute of God shines brighter in the Old Testament than does His patience, particularly His forbearance with Israel. "The Lord your God is God, *the faithful God who keeps covenant* and steadfast love with those who love him and keep his commandments," Moses reminded Israel before his death in the land of Moab (Deuteronomy 7:9, emphasis added).

Moses knew well the numerous times Israel had tried the Lord's patience. When, on the borders of Canaan, the people turned into a hysterical, rampaging mob over the discouraging report of the ten spies, he had earnestly prayed, "Let the power of the Lord be great as thou hast promised, saying, 'The Lord is *slow to anger*, and abounding in steadfast love, forgiving iniquity and transgression' . . . as thou hast forgiven this people, from Egypt even until now" (Numbers 14:17-19, emphasis added). Ezekiel, too, the prophet of the captivity, traced for the exiles around him on the Chebar Canal the long history of God's patience with the nation (see Ezekiel 20).

But God's patience is not indulgence—not loud threats followed by winking at Israel's repeated apostasies until (like some parents) He loses His temper (humanly speaking) and acts rashly. The Lord is not capricious (see Numbers 23:19). He deals with the sin problem and with His people in harmony with His righteous character. "All his ways are justice. A God of faithfulness and without iniquity, just and right is he" (Deuteronomy 32:4). On this point the prophet himself needed instruction, and the Lord sent him as a pupil to a potter's shop in Jerusalem.

Parable of the potter

Pottery making is an ancient craft. Because of its distinctive cultural shapes and its indestructibility, earthenware is an important tool in archaeological research for dating excavation levels in Palestine, where written materials are practically nonexistent. Pottery dating has become a science and is more accurate than most would think possible.

"Arise, and go down to the potter's house, and there I will let you hear my words," the Lord directed Jeremiah. The prophet obeyed and found the potter "working at his wheel" (Jeremiah 18:2, 3).

The potter's wheel, sometimes called a "kick wheel," consisted of two wheels (stone or wood), the larger fitted on the lower end of a vertical, standing axle, and the smaller on the upper end. When the potter sat before the device and turned the lower wheel with his feet, the upper wheel on which he threw his clay would spin, enabling the potter to shape the mass with both hands.

As Jeremiah watched, something went wrong. "The vessel he was making of clay was spoiled in the potter's hand, and he reworked it into another vessel, as it seemed good to the potter to do" (verse 4). This was the point God wanted Jeremiah to grasp: the potter controlled the clay. If he did not succeed in his first attempt, he began again. In the object lesson of the shattered flask (see Jeremiah 19), the clay had been fired; it was too late for national change.

But in the potter's parable, the clay was still plastic and could still be worked, symbolizing that a new start could still be made. Chronologically, Jeremiah's visit to the potter's shop must have taken place early in the reign of Jehoiakim, when repentance and reformation were still possible.

The truth of God's sovereignty over the human race—as a potter has "authority" over his clay—arises from the Creation account itself, in which the Creator *formed* (*yāsar*) "man of dust from the ground" (Genesis 2:7). Isaiah acknowledged God as the master Potter: "O Lord, thou art our Father; we are the clay, and thou art our *potter* [*yôsēr*]; we are all the work of thy hand" (Isaiah 64:8, emphasis added). And Jeremiah, having watched a *potter* (*yôsēr*) rework his lump and begin again to shape it into a useful piece, heard God speak: "The word of the Lord came to me: 'O house of Israel, can I not do with you as this potter has done? . . . Behold, like the clay in the potter's hand, so are you in my hand' " (Jeremiah 18:6). Both God and the potter exercised sovereign control over their respective "clays." The potter attempted to make a vessel with his lump, but the process was marred. So *he* (not the clay) chose to rework the lump. In like manner, God had attempted to make Israel into a vessel of glory and honor, but the nation marred itself in God's hands, as it were. Now, He wished to try again.

But the illustration has its limits. The clay is inanimate. It has no will of its own and cannot resist the determined purpose of the craftsman. Human beings, on the other hand, were created as free moral agents. Although God is sovereign, He does not override the human will.

This "real life" parable of the potter led the Lord to make one of the great summary statements of Scripture. This statement explains the principle by which He deals with the human race. The full statement is worth contemplating: "*If* at any time I declare concerning a nation or a kingdom, that I will pluck up and break down and destroy it, and *if* that nation, concerning which I have spoken, turns from its evil, I will repent of the evil that I intended to do to it. And *if* at any time I declare concerning a nation or a kingdom that I will build and plant it, and *if* it does evil in my sight, not listening to my voice, *then* I will repent of the good which I had intended to do to it" (verses 7-10, emphasis added).

The "if," "if," "then" sequence—twice given—plainly indicates that the fulfillment of divine pronouncements of judgment or blessing are *conditional on the human response.* If judgment is threatened and sinners repent, God calls off the judgment; if blessing is promised, but sinners choose to live in disobedience, the blessing is withheld.[1] God is sovereign, but He forces no one. He acknowledges each person's free will, his or her right of choice to obey or to reject Him. Our eternal destiny—corporate and individual—is determined by our choices.[2]

At this point in Judah's experience, the nation apparently was still like plastic clay on the potter's wheel. Although marred by its idolatry and apostasy, the nation was not yet beyond the divine Potter's skill to make it into a vessel of beauty and usefulness. But unlike the clay, Judah would have *to choose* to submit to His will. That is one obvious message of the parable. But God couches His message to the people from another angle, making a play on the potter's craft: "Now, therefore, say to the men of Judah . . . 'Thus says the Lord, Behold, I am *shaping* [yôsēr] evil against you and devising a plan against you. *Return*, every one from his evil way, and *amend* your ways and your doings' " (verse 11, emphasis added). It is absolutely clear that the nation could, indeed, determine its own destiny.

But the golden moment of repentance and renewal was ignored. God knew their answer. "But they say, 'That is in vain! We will follow our own plans, and will every one act according to the stubbornness of his evil heart' " (verse 12).

Temple theology

If we read the writings of Jeremiah carefully—between the lines, as it were—we sense that a basic cause of his conflict with the priests and false prophets lay in their different theological views of the covenant.[3] The opposing positions have a definite relationship to the parable of the potter.

The conflict may be summed up under this simple rubric— "temple theology." The contention surfaces in Jeremiah's famous "temple sermon" (see Jeremiah 7:1-6; 26:1-24), in which the prophet warned: "Do not trust in these deceptive words: 'This is the temple of the Lord, the temple of the Lord, the temple of the Lord' " (Jeremiah 7:4).

Jeremiah's opponents reasoned something like this: (1) Had God chosen Zion/Jerusalem as His permanent dwelling place? Yes, for it was written: "The Lord has chosen Zion; he has desired it for his habitation: 'This is my resting place for ever' " (Psalm 132:13, 14). (2) Had God chosen the temple to place His name there forever? Yes, for it was written: "I have consecrated this house which you [Solomon] have built, and put my name there for ever; my eyes and my heart will be there for all time" (1 Kings 9:3). (3) Did God protect both the city and temple from Assyrian destruction in the reign of Hezekiah? Yes, for it was written: "Thus says the Lord concerning the king of Assyria, He shall not come into this city or shoot an arrow there, or come before it with a shield or cast up a siege mound against it. . . . For I will defend this city to save it, for my own sake and for the sake of my servant David" (2 Kings 19:32-34). (4) Did God promise David an everlasting dynasty? Yes, for it was written: "Your house and your kingdom shall be made sure for ever before me; your throne shall be established for ever" (2 Samuel 7:16).

In sum, the priest's temple theology rested on the premise that God's promises were *unconditional*—no conditions attached. God had promised everlasting permanence to the Davidic throne, Jerusalem, and the temple. God, as a Father, might discipline His people from time to time, but He would never permit total destruction to these three institutions. Therefore, Jeremiah was wrong to preach their complete ruin. God would never allow it.

Jeremiah's temple theology was just the opposite. In effect, he argued that God's promises were entirely *conditional* on Judah's obedience to God's will. Transgression nullified the divine promises. "Go now to my place that was in Shiloh, where I made my name dwell at first, and see what I did to it for the wickedness of my people Israel," God instructed Jeremiah to say (Jeremiah 7:12). The tabernacle was pitched in Shiloh after Israel's conquest of Canaan under Joshua's leadership. At this central location in the tribe of Ephraim, the tribes worshiped until God permitted the destruction of the city and the capture of the ark by the Philistines in the days of Eli.

God's message to Judah via the potter's work exposed the theological delusion that priest and false prophet had embraced. God's promises of permanence for the temple, Jerusalem, and the Davidic dynasty—the "good" He intended for the nation—were thus conditional on national obedience to divine authority. The Lord's patience, His long-suffering, might be misread, might seem to deny the conditional nature of these promises, but to think otherwise was to misunderstand the nature of His grace (see Jeremiah 18:9, 10).

God could not make the principles by which He operates more plain. "If you will not listen to me, to walk in my law which I have set before you, . . . *then I will make this house like Shiloh, and I will make this city a curse for all the nations of the earth*" (Jeremiah 26: 4-6, emphasis added). Ezekiel administered the *coup de grâce* by announcing later, to the Jews in exile, the downfall of the Davidic dynasty (see Ezekiel 21:25-27).

Breaking the barriers

The key to a new start—to a new spiritual experience—is to break the barriers of sin that separate you from God. As the shadows lengthened on Judah's day of probation, God spoke to His people through Jeremiah: "Break up your fallow ground, and sow not among thorns" (Jeremiah 4:3). Fallow ground is cultivated land that is left idle during the growing season. The land's condition is indicated in the second line of the couplet: "sow not among *thorns*." As anyone knows who has left a previous garden plot unattended, the next season some edible plants will sprout from seeds dropped at harvesttime, but mostly weeds and thorns will spring up in the neglected plot.

Jesus may have drawn on Jeremiah's figure when He told the parable of the Sower (see Mark 4:3-20). In Jesus' parable, the thorns are identified as "the cares of the world, and the delight in riches, and the desire for other things" (verse 19). In Jeremiah's time, the "thorns" would have symbolized the unnatural implantation of foreign deities and the resultant gross practices and apostasy that had choked out the worship of the true God.

The appeal is often made today: "Just believe on Jesus as your Saviour and Lord—just believe, and you will be accounted righteous in Him." This is grand news, but it is deceptive when it is disconnected from genuine repentance and confession of sin. If the penitent sinner truly receives Jesus Christ into his or her life, the plowshare of divine grace will be allowed to tear up the soil and uproot the thorns and weeds of sin. Repentance is a genuine work of grace (see Acts 5:31; 2:37, 38). Its absence—and lack of confession (1 John 1:9)—leaves the fallow heart untouched and aborts the salvation process.[4]

Jeremiah also employed the sign of covenant fidelity—circumcision—to express the need to remove sin's barriers. "Circumcise yourselves to the Lord, remove the foreskin of your hearts, O men of Judah and inhabitants of Jerusalem" (Jeremiah 4:4).

Originally, circumcision functioned as a visible token (in the flesh) of the covenant relationship between God and Abraham and the latter's descendants. (see Genesis 17:11-13). Paul also interpreted circumcision "as a sign or seal of the righteousness which [Abraham] had by faith" (Romans 4:11).

Early on, however, the foreskin acquired the spiritual symbolism of an impediment. For example, Moses sought to evade God's call to leadership by claiming to be "a man of uncircumcised lips" (Exodus 6:12, 30). For some reason—physically or spiritually, he felt that his lips were encased or sealed over. But more commonly the foreskin symbolized an impediment to the proper function of the *heart*—the Hebrew term for the mind and all the aspects of the human intelligence.

When Jeremiah appealed to Judah to circumcise the heart, he repeated the command of Moses: "Circumcise therefore the foreskin of your *heart*, and be no longer stubborn" (Deuteronomy 10:16, emphasis added; see also chapter 50:6). The foreskin of the heart symbolized Judah's stubborn sinfulness, which, like a tight band of superfluous flesh, prevented God's people from serving Him with all their devotion. The New Testament plainly identifies the symbol as "the body of the sins of the flesh," which is removed by Christ (Colossians 2:11, NKJV).

Jeremiah applied the same figure to the ear. "Behold, their ears are closed [literally, "uncircumcised"], they cannot listen; behold, the word of the Lord is to them an object of scorn, they take no pleasure in it" (Jeremiah 6:10). Judah's spiritual ears were blocked; the spiritual hearts were encased in their sinful ways. Circumcised in the physical flesh, but not in the spiritual heart and ear, they would die in the same judgment that would fall on the uncircumcised nations around them unless they repented (see Jeremiah 9:25, 26).

The appeal of Jeremiah chapter 4, verses 1 to 4 came during the reign of Josiah. At the outset of Jehoiakim's reign, Jeremiah repeated God's admonition in his dynamic temple sermon. "Amend your ways and your doings, and I will let you dwell in this place" (Jeremiah 7:3). He then listed the areas of their lives that needed serious reform (verses 5, 6).

But by the time of Jehoiachin and Zedekiah, the national character appeared to be fixed. "Can the Ethiopian change his skin or the leopard his spots? Then also you can do good who are accustomed to do evil?" (Jeremiah 13:23).[5] Judah's opportunity for removing the barriers of sin was gone; only "a fearful prospect of judgment" remained (see Hebrews 10:27).

Turning tragedy to triumph

Tragedy marked the year 597 B.C. for Jerusalem—or so it seemed. Baited by Jehoiakim's revolt against the crown a few years earlier (see 2 Kings 24:1), Nebuchadnezzar eventually invaded Judah in the spring of that year and took Jerusalem on March 16, according to the Babylonian Chronicle. Jehoiakim was dead, but the victorious Babylonians took his young son, King Jehoiachin, and his family, along with ten thousand of the best citizens— princes, warriors, craftsmen—into captivity, reducing the population to "the poorest people of the land" (see 2 Kings 24:8-16). Zedekiah, another of Josiah's sons, was placed as a puppet ruler on the throne of the impoverished state (verses 17, 18).

The swiftness of the invasion and siege (see verse 11) must have traumatized the national spirit. But the pundits—priests and false prophets—calmed the people with the usual panaceas; conventional wisdom argued that the judgment of deportation had fallen without question on the greatest sinners among them. But though the sobbing captives could not see it, this was the Lord's design for a new start.

The Lord explained the situation to Jeremiah in a graphic vision: "Behold, two baskets of figs placed before the temple of the Lord. One basket had very good figs, like the first-ripe figs, but the other basket had very bad figs, so bad that they could not be eaten" (Jeremiah 24:1, 2). Then God astonished the prophet with His next statement: *"Like these good figs, so I will regard as good the exiles from Judah, whom I have sent away from this place to the land of the Chaldeans"* (verse 5, emphasis added).

Jehoiachin (Jeconiah), his court, and most of the ten thousand captives were largely idolaters like their counterparts left behind. But God separated them from the mass and moved them away from the approaching terrors of the sword and final siege. This apparent tragedy would turn to triumph. From this group and their descendants, God would form a new Israel, who would continue to uphold His name in the earth and through whom the Messiah would come.

God explained in more detail: "I will set my eyes upon them for good." "I will bring them back to this land . . . [and] build them up." "I will give them a heart to know [Me]." "They shall be my people and I will be their God." "They shall return to me with their whole heart" (verses 6, 7). God foresaw that the hope of an Israelite future lay with a remnant of this group—disciplined by the captivity.

Jeremiah later wrote an encouraging letter to these exiles, counseling them to settle down, build houses, plant gardens, marry and preserve their numbers, and seek the peace of the cities in which they were scattered until the time came for their release. God assured them through the prophet: "You will seek me and find me; when you seek me with all your heart, I will be found by you, says the Lord, and I will restore your fortunes and gather you from all the nations and all the places where I have driven you, says the Lord, and I will bring you back to the place from which I sent you into exile" (Jeremiah 29:13, 14).

The basket of bad figs represented Zedekiah, his princes, and the rest of the people who remained in the land. They learned nothing from the humiliation of the invasion of 597 B.C. A few years later, Zedekiah and his sin-hardened princes—seized with delusions of power—led Judah in one more revolt against Nebuchadnezzar, only to be crushed with untold cruelty and suffering by the iron heel of the conqueror (see Jeremiah 24:8-10).

The vision of the two baskets of figs is a true sequel to the parable of the potter. Without violating the free will of the Judaists, the Lord permitted Babylon's second invasion to separate the people. In this manner the master Potter reworked His clay and cast it upon the wheel of the Babylonian captivity to shape and to form a new Israel. The intransigence of humans cannot prevent the Sovereign Ruler from carrying out His eternal purpose. From the "good fig" remnant would eventually come the Messiah, the world's Saviour!

---

1. See Jonah 3:10. Nineveh's repentance, in response to Jonah's preaching of imminent judgment, canceled the destruction.

2. To say that God "repents" is to use an anthropomorphic term to describe an action of the Deity. But it is evident from the passage that God's so-called repentance is not the same as human repentance. God is "without iniquity" and, consequently, has no need of repentance as human beings do (see Deuteronomy 32:4). Since Jeremiah 18:7-10 notes that God repented of "good" as well as "evil," it is clear that His "repentance" means the kind of response He makes to human choices. The variable in God's promises and judgments always lies in the human reaction to His announcement of them.

3. *ISBE*, 2:986, 987.

4. See Ellen G. White, *Selected Messages* (Washington, D.C.: Review and Herald Publishing Association, 1958), bk. 2, 19.

5. Removed from its context, Jeremiah 13:23 can be construed to state a universal truth that no power resides within the sinner to effect a change of heart. God's grace alone can change the inner life and bring about "new birth" (see John 3:5-8; 2 Corinthians 5:17). However, in its context the passage appears to state the hopeless condition of Judah, who had passed her day of grace.

Chapter 8
Sabbath Sacredness

"Go and stand at the gate of the people, through which the kings of Judah go in and out; stand also at all the other gates of Jerusalem," the Lord ordered Jeremiah one day (Jeremiah 17:19, NIV). In the time of the Judaist monarchy, Jerusalem had seven gates. City gates in Near Eastern cities were the common centers for business: buying and selling, as well as public hearings, legal transactions, civil trials, etc. (see 2 Kings 7:1; Ruth 4:1-12). It is not certain which of the gates was used by the monarch and his court. But since the prophet's message on this occasion related to Jerusalem's commercial life, it is evident that he moved about from gate to gate to speak to the businessmen and their employees.

Jeremiah 17:19-27 deals with the subject of Sabbath observance by the business segment of the populace. The prophet has already spoken pointedly about Judah's gross idolatry and covenant breaking, violations of the first and second precepts of the Decalogue. Why should he not be directed by God to speak out about the national violations of the fourth precept? Consequently, we must interpret Jeremiah's presentation of the Sabbath—unpack its brief summarization—in the light of Mosaic teachings, the scriptural backdrop for his message.

The worship of Yahweh had become only a form. The true God was worshiped alongside a pantheon of pagan gods. For all practical purposes, the Sabbath had become a regular business day. Jeremiah addressed the rulers and laborers together: "Take heed for the sake of your lives, and do not bear a burden on the sabbath day or bring it in by the gates of Jerusalem. And do not carry a burden out of your houses on the sabbath or do any work, but keep the sabbath day holy, as I commanded your fathers" (Jeremiah 17:21, 22).

Jeremiah describes a scene of active buying and trading. The traffic into the city brought produce from the fields—wine, grain, figs, grapes, and other agricultural products (see Nehemiah 13:15 for a similar experience). The "burdens" the people brought from their houses may have been manufactured goods to be sold or bartered for the produce in the city's bazaars.

The messages about the Sabbath (chapter 17) and the potter's activity (chapter 18) are thought to have been spoken in the first part of Jehoiakim's reign, when the possibilities for repentance still existed. Both messages touch on the *conditional* nature of God's threatened judgments or promised blessings (see Jeremiah 17:24-27; 18:7-10). The ultimate results are determined by the human response. In chapter 17 two conditions are proclaimed: the first, positive; the second, negative.

1. "If you listen to me, says the Lord, and bring in no burden by the gates of this city on the sabbath day, but keep the sabbath day holy and do no work on it, *then* there shall enter by the gates of this city kings who sit on the throne of David, riding in chariots and on horses, they and their princes, the men of Judah and the inhabitants of Jerusalem; *and this city shall be inhabited for ever*" (verses 24, 25, emphasis added).

Jeremiah's exclamation, "This city shall be inhabited for ever," must have thrilled him as much as it electrified his hearers! Jerusalem, the eternal city! "The perfection of beauty, the joy of all the earth" (Lamentations 2:15)! The scene rose before the prophet's wondering eyes: "People shall come from the cities of Judah and the places round about Jerusalem, from the land of Benjamin, from the Shephelah, from the hill country, and from the Negeb, bringing burnt offerings and sacrifices, cereal offerings, and frankincense and bringing thank offerings to the house of the Lord" (verse 26). What magnificent possibilities lay before Judah!

2. But Jeremiah had to also warn his commercially active audiences of the negative possibility as well: "But *if* you do not listen to me, to keep the sabbath day holy, and not to bear a burden and enter by the gates of Jerusalem on the sabbath day, *then* I will kindle a fire in its gates, and it shall devour the palaces of Jerusalem and shall not be quenched" (verse 27, emphasis added). It was not necessary to add what any hardheaded businessman among them would know: that the ruin of the city/nation meant the ruin of business and the collapse of personal fortunes.

The promised blessing of a flourishing city and nation, praising God from whom all blessings flowed, or a dire threat of ruin—each scenario depended on Judah's choice.

But what is so significant about the observance of the Sabbath—or its nonobservance—that either could bring about such weal or woe to God's professing people? The answer lies once more in Judah's covenant relationship with God and the instruction God gave to His servant Moses. In this instance, Jeremiah could have accommodated the words of Jesus, had He lived earlier: "If you believed Moses, you would believe me. . . . But if you do not believe his writings, how will you believe my words?" (John 5:46, 47).

Old Testament testimony to the Sabbath

The institution of the seventh-day Sabbath as a holy day for spiritual rest and renewal is recorded in Genesis 2:2, 3. Apart from its institution, Moses employs the word *Sabbath* for the seventh-day rest, in eleven passages: four each in Exodus (16; 20; 31; 35) and Leviticus (19; 23; 24; 26), twice in Numbers (15; 28); and once in Deuteronomy (5). Exodus 20:8-11 and Deuteronomy 5:12-14 state the fourth precept of the Ten Commandments, but Exodus 31:13-17 provides the most extensive statement on the meaning of the Sabbath in the entire Old Testament.

When Jeremiah appealed to the laborers and businessmen of Judah to "keep the sabbath day holy, *as I commanded your fathers*" (Jeremiah 17:22, emphasis added), he alluded to Exodus 31 as well as to the fourth precept and other briefer counsels. This same comprehensive statement is obviously the basis for Ezekiel's comments about the Sabbath that he made to the Jewish exiles in Babylonia (see Ezekiel 20:12, 20). We will need to briefly study this foundational passage (see Exodus 31:13-17).

The Creator's sign

The hosts of Israel lay encamped before Mt. Sinai. Just prior to the construction of the tabernacle, the Lord gave Moses instruction for the people about the significance of the Sabbath. Three great truths were touched on: *creation*, *salvation*, and *security*.

Six days shall work be done, but the seventh day is a sabbath of solemn rest, holy to the Lord. . . . It is a *sign* for ever between me and the people of Israel that in six days the Lord made heaven and earth, and on the seventh day he rested, and was refreshed (Exodus 31:15-17, emphasis added).

The Hebrew word for "sign" (*'ôth*) has a variety of nuances. It can refer to a pledge or token, an omen, a symbol, or a miracle. And it may also be used in the sense of a memorial or an ensign. By calling the observance of the Sabbath a "sign," God designated it as a badge of loyalty, a distinguishing token or mark that would set Israel apart from all other peoples as the worshipers of Yahweh, the Creator of heaven and earth (see Ezekiel 20:20). To date there is no archaeological evidence that other nations of antiquity recognized a weekly Sabbath as a regular religious day of rest.[1]

At least four times Jeremiah refers to the Lord as the Creator. "The Lord is the true God; he is the living God. . . . It is he who made the earth" (Jeremiah 10:10-12; see also chapters 27:4, 5; 32:17; 51:14, 15). A Judaist might give *mental assent* to the belief that Yahweh was the Creator (as the fourth commandment reads— Exodus 20:8-11), and no one would know the difference. But the moment he *observed* the seventh-day Sabbath as a holy day of worship, ceasing his labor by which he made his livelihood, he became a marked man in the eyes of his pagan neighbors. The observance of the Sabbath thus functioned as a waving banner. It made a believer in the true God stand out—to be counted![2]

The observer of the Sabbath acknowledges a number of important truths—valid in present times as in Jeremiah's. For example, when the observer recognizes Yahweh as a *personal* God, who made the human race in His image (see Genesis 1:26, 27), he denies pagan myths of origin. Humanity came from the hand of the living, personal Creator, who designed His creation—not leaving it to evolve by chance.

The observer of the seventh-day Sabbath is not troubled with those so-called "night questions" some lie awake pondering: "Where did I come from?" "Why am I here?" "Why the human predicament?" "What is the meaning and purpose of my life?" "What happens when I die?" The Sabbath memorial testifies that the Creator has a purpose and plan for His earth-bound creatures (see Isaiah 45:18; Revelation 4:11). In His Word (the Holy Bible), the Creator explains His intent in creation, how sin originated and marred His plan, but how Heaven has devised and is carrying out a far-reaching plan for human salvation.

One great truth that the Sabbath observer confesses is his or her absolute dependence upon the Creator for life itself as well as for physical and spiritual care (see Acts 17:28). In contrast, the attitude of many others is: " I can take care of myself. I can make a living with my own hands and brain and enjoy as much material good as I can obtain. And If I need to work seven days a week, I'll do it. I have no need of God!"

The modern urbanite can scarcely grasp the conditions of agrarian societies that lie beyond twentieth-century technology. For a Sabbath keeper in such a culture—and in Palestine of antiquity—to cease labor each week for a twenty-four-hour period in order to devote quality time to the worship of God and to spiritual concerns takes great faith and trust. Humanly speaking, it is contrary to common sense. Every farmer must take advantage of every day of good weather he has, if he is to succeed—so conventional wisdom would argue.

But in God's government of Israel and Judah, even agriculture's busiest seasons were not to interrupt the weekly observance of the Sabbath. God commanded: "Six days you shall work, but on the seventh day you shall rest; *in plowing time and in harvest you shall rest*" (Exodus 34:21, emphasis added). It took a sturdy faith to believe that God would guarantee agricultural success when, during these important seasons, farm work was laid aside for spiritual pursuits! Life depended on God's promises.

It takes great faith today to live committed to the will of the Creator. Jesus recognized this fundamental dependence that every believer acknowledges when he/she steps out of the crowd to obey the heavenly Father's will. He assured, "Do not be anxious, saying, 'What shall we eat?' or 'What shall we drink?' or 'What shall we wear?' For the Gentiles seek all these things; and your heavenly Father knows that you need them all. But seek first his kingdom and his righteousness, and all these things shall be yours as well" (Matthew 6:31-33).

Sabbath observance was one of the strongest means of grace in the Old Testament era in that it kept the focus of faith on the true God, the Creator—the Source and Sustainer of all life. It undergirded the first two precepts of the Decalogue, which prohibited idolatry. The abandonment of the Sabbath—turning it into an ordinary working day—contributed to the withering of a true knowledge of Yahweh and made easier Judah's avid embracing of pagan deities.

The Sanctifier's sign

Beyond the assurance of the Creator's care, the Sabbath carried another special communication to the Israelites. The Lord said to Moses: "Say to the people of Israel, 'You shall keep my sabbaths, for this is a *sign* between me and you throughout your generations, that you may know that I, the Lord, *sanctify* you' " (Exodus 31:12, emphasis added; see also Ezekiel 20:12). The Hebrew participle that describes God as Israel's "Sanctifier" comes from the verb root *qdš*, meaning "to be set apart, consecrated." The participle describes God as "keeping his people pure and sacred."[3]

Just as the public observance of the Sabbath was a badge of an Israelite's loyalty to Yahweh, the Creator of heaven and earth—which loyalty the pagan could see—so its observance reminded the Israelite that Yahweh had separated him and his nation from all other peoples, consecrating them to Himself.

Moses reminded Israel of this significant fact just before he died: "You are a people *holy* to the Lord your God; the Lord your God has chosen you to be a people for his own possession, out of all the peoples that are on the face of the earth" (Deuteronomy 7:6, emphasis added). By means of His deliverance from Egyptian slavery, the Lord set Israel apart for Himself.

But the divine Sanctifier had more in mind than physical freedom. "You shall be *holy*; for I the Lord your God am *holy*" (Leviticus 19:2, emphasis added), God repeated several times to the nation. The word *holy* derives from the same Hebrew root as does the verb *to sanctify*. But in this passage *holy* shades off from the basic idea of separation to the idea of morality. As the "Holy One" of Israel (see Isaiah 6:3), God is not only separate from humans, but He is separate from their infirmaries, impurities, and sins. And as He is morally holy, so His people are called to separate themselves from all sin and impurity. How is this to be done?

Perhaps it can be best understood in its Old Testament setting if we briefly examine the Bible's several models of the nature of sin. These are found mainly in the New Testament. For example:

1. Sin may be defined as "the transgression of the law" (1 John 3:4, KJV) or "lawlessness" (RSV). As such, sin must be "propitiated" (1 John 2:2, KJV) or "expiated" (RSV).

2. Sin may be viewed as a "debt" (Matthew 6:12), for which "forgiveness" is sought (Matthew 18:27).

3. Sin may be defined as "slavery" (John 8:34), freedom from

which requires a "ransom" to be paid (Matthew 20:28).

4. Sin may be understood as an "estrangement" between God and human beings (2 Corinthians 5:18-20). This situation calls for a mediator to assist in bringing about "reconciliation" (Romans 5:10).

5. In contrast, the Old Testament tends to describe sin as an inner uncleanness (see Isaiah 6:5), a corruption of the heart/mind (Jeremiah 17:9), an inner rebellion and insensitivity (see Ezekiel 36:26). Little wonder, in light of these descriptions of the corrupt and deceitful nature of the carnal mind with its natural bent to sin, that the apostle Paul cried out: "Wretched man that I am! Who will deliver me from *this body of death*?" (Romans 7:25, emphasis added).

Repentant David showed sinful Judah the way out when he sought forgiveness and restoration himself: "*Purge* me with hyssop [the blood of the Passover lamb, hyssop-sprinkled on the door posts, diverted the death angel in Egypt], and I shall be clean; *wash* me, and I shall be whiter than snow. . . . *Create in me a clean heart, O God, and put a right spirit within me*" (Psalm 51:7-10, emphasis added).

God *sanctifies* His people—whether they be Judaists of antiquity or believers today—through His forgiving grace and creative power that gives them "clean" hearts, "new" hearts, and "right" spirits *within*, so that they may be able to say with the Messiah: "I delight to do thy will, O my God; thy law is within my heart" (Psalm 40:8).

It is evident that after the Fall, the observance of the Sabbath took on an added meaning. Not only did it distinguish observers as worshipers of the true God, who created the heavens and earth, but it also assured the observers themselves that the same Creator would re-create their inner lives, enabling them to live as holy people. Thus, the Sabbath became—and remains—a sign or pledge by God of the believer's salvation from sin's dominion and blight.

Sign of security

Once more God underlined the significance of the Sabbath by saying through Moses: "The people of Israel shall keep the sabbath, observing the sabbath throughout their generations, as a *perpetual* ['ôlām, "everlasting"] covenant" (Exodus 31:16, emphasis added).

It may appear at first that God viewed the institution of the Sabbath as a covenant separate from the one He made with Israel at Sinai. But the Bible writers designate any part of the biblical covenant as the covenant itself (for example, God's promises are called the covenant, Galatians 3:16, 17, as are the Ten Commandments, Deuteronomy 4:13, and the Messiah Himself, Isaiah 42:6).

Consequently, the Sabbath is not the full covenant itself, but simply serves as another sign of the covenant God made with His people. It might be said that "circumcision" was an "internal," hidden sign of covenant loyalty, whereas the observance of the Sabbath was an "external," open sign of the covenant.

Circumcision, a part of the ritual requirements, came many years after the Fall and was given to Abraham and his descendants as a badge of their loyalty to God. The Sabbath, on the other hand, was instituted in Eden *before* the entrance of sin by the act of the Creator Himself, who "rested" on the seventh day of Creation week, blessed the day, and set it apart for holy observance by the human family (see Genesis 2:2, 3). As Jesus later declared: "The sabbath was made for man," that is to say, the Sabbath was made for the sake of man, for the blessing of human beings (Mark 2:27). The fourth precept, commanding its observance, was enshrined in the heart of the moral law of the Ten Commandments, the permanent law of God that defines our duties to the Creator and to one another (see Exodus 20:8-11).

Thus, when the "new covenant" was confirmed at Calvary and the ceremonial system—including circumcision—dropped away, the Sabbath continued to remain an external sign of the believer's covenant relationship to his Creator and Sanctifier. As long as the fact remains that God made this earth and the human family by fiat in six days, so long will the seventh-day Sabbath remain as a memorial of that great event. Thus, the Sabbath becomes to the believer a sign of his security. He is God's property, His special possession, by right of creation and redemption (see 1 Corinthians 6:19, 20). He is God's covenant partner.

Why did Judah, in the times of Jeremiah, ignore the observance of the Sabbath? Why did they desecrate its holy hours with commercial transactions (Jeremiah 17:21, 22)? Did they fear possible food shortages if they did not take advantage of the Sabbath hours for agricultural pursuits? Or, did the observance of the Sabbath embarrass them in their business dealings with their pagan neighbors? But the bottom line registers the hard facts: Judah no longer loved and trusted the Creator.

Sign of release

Though the Sabbath was set aside by the Creator as a day of spiritual and physical rest for all humankind, Jeremiah knew from his reading of "the book of the law" that it held special significance for Israel. In repeating the Ten Commandments to the national assembly in Moab, Moses had reminded them that the Sabbath rest was for the benefit of their servants too. Then he added this significant reminder: "You shall remember that you were a servant in the land of Egypt, and the Lord your God brought you out thence with a mighty hand and an outstretched arm; therefore the Lord your God commanded you to keep the sabbath day" (Deuteronomy 5:15).

Israel lived in Egypt for several hundred years. During the latter part of their sojourn, they were cruelly enslaved. The Egyptians "made their lives bitter with hard service, in mortar and brick, and in all kinds of work in the field; in all their work they made them serve with rigor" (Exodus 1:14). Such toil—driven by demanding taskmasters—probably prevented any kind of regular Sabbath keeping.[4] The future was bleak, especially after the pharaoh began a program of genocide.

But their covenant-keeping God had not forgotten them! "I have remembered my covenant," He said to the people. "I will bring you out from under the burdens of the Egyptians, and I will deliver you from their bondage, and I will redeem you with an outstretched arm and with great acts of judgment, and I will take you for my people, and I will be your God; and you shall know that I am the Lord your God" (Exodus 6:6, 7).

We wonder how Judah could ever forget such lavish favor! But to the Jews living in Jeremiah's time—nearly nine hundred years distant from the great deliverance out of slavery—it was all a very dim tale. Times were different now, they probably said.

Times would, indeed, be different! Jerusalem—its temple, palaces, and homes—a holocaust (see Jeremiah 17:27)! Judah—decimated by sword, famine, and pestilence—deported into captivity. Foolish Judah!—to exchange the rest of the Sabbath (that signified their bond to the eternal Creator, Saviour, and their security) for a hectic life of relentless toil and in the end the loss of everything! Jesus summarized this kind of situation with a penetrating question: "What will it profit a man, if he gains the whole world and forfeits his life?" (Matthew 16:26).

1. *SDABD*, s.v. "Sabbath," 961.

2. "The Sabbath is a pledge given by God to man—a sign of the relation existing between the Creator and His created beings. By observing the memorial of the creation of the world in six days and the rest of the Creator on the seventh day, by keeping the Sabbath holy, according to His directions, the Israelites were to declare to the world their loyalty to the only true and living God, the Sovereign of the universe" (Ellen G. White, *Selected Messages* [Washington, D.C.: Review and Herald Publishing Association, 1980], 3:256).

3. Francis Brown, S. R. Driver, and Charles A. Briggs, eds, *A Hebrew and English Lexicon of the Old Testament*, s.v. "qdš" (Boston and New York: Houghton Mifflin Company, 1907), 871-874.

4. "In their bondage the Israelites had to some extent lost the knowledge of God's law, and they had departed from its precepts. The Sabbath had been generally disregarded, and the exactions of their taskmasters made its observance apparently impossible" (White, *Patriarchs and Prophets*, 258).

Chapter 9

Divine Discipline

"The Lord laid me on my back so that He could look me in the face," an acquaintance of mine said with a twinkle in his eye. The imagery conjures up many possible scenarios, such as a wrestler throwing my friend and pinning his shoulders to the mat! But in this instance, the severe discipline of disease had laid him helpless on a hospital bed with time to think about the meaning of life. The Lord overruled his tragedy "for good" (Romans 8:28), and he came to know his Saviour in a more intimate relationship.

The Sovereign of the universe has a concern for the peoples of earth, because they come from His creative hand (see Acts 17: 24-27). Like a father, He pities the sinful race, especially those who acknowledge Him as Lord (see Psalm 103:13). That pity—His love—must at times discipline them for their good (see Hebrews 12:5-11). Judah was no exception.

The death of Josiah (608 B.C.) signaled the beginning of the last two decades of Judah's national existence. It was time for God to lay before His people His specific plans for their future, although appeals for repentance would continue.

In 605 B.C. (Jehoiakim's third regnal year and Nebuchadnezzar's accession year), the Babylonians invaded Judah for the first time, briefly besieged Jerusalem, and took hostages from the royal and noble families, together with a quantity of gold and silver vessels from the temple (see Daniel 1:1-4; 5:2).

The following year, 604 B.C. (Jehoiakim's fourth and Nebuchadnezzar's first), Jeremiah candidly addressed the nation (see Jeremiah 25). He reminded them that for twenty-three years his "persistent" appeals had fallen on deaf ears. Furthermore, God had sent other prophets as well (verses 1-5).[1] All presented the same earnest entreaty to repent of their idolatry (verses 5, 6).

Next, Jeremiah proceeded to announce God's intention to permit Nebuchadnezzar, king of Babylon, and the forces of the countries in league with him to conquer Judah and the surrounding nations.[2] "I will utterly destroy them, and make them a horror, a hissing, and an *everlasting* [*ôlām*] reproach. . . . This whole land shall become a ruin and a waste, and these nations shall serve the king of Babylon *seventy years*" (verses 9-11, emphasis added).[3]

The seventy-year captivity

After Nebuchadnezzar's second major invasion, at which time he deported King Jehoiachin and ten thousand captives to Babylon (597 B.C.), the Lord again affirmed the length of the exile: "When *seventy years* are completed for Babylon, I will visit you, and I will fulfil to you my promise and bring you back to this place" (Jeremiah 29:10, emphasis added).

There is no reason for not accepting this twice-stated period of seventy years as literal time. While scholars speculate on its beginning and ending dates, it is most easily understood as the period extending from the exiling of the first hostages in 605 B.C. (Daniel, his close associates, and others) through the next two major invasions and deportations (597 B.C., 588-586 B.C.) until the appearance in Palestine of the first wave of repatriates in 536 B.C. under the governorship of Zerubbabel with Joshua the high priest. Counting inclusively from 605 B.C. to 536 B.C. gives a period of seventy years.

Several reasons were probably factored into the Lord's determination to extend the exile for seventy years. Surprisingly, one of these appears to have been ecological! "Six years you shall sow your field, and six years you shall prune your vineyard, and gather in its fruits," God had instructed Israel, "but in the seventh year there shall be *a sabbath of solemn rest for the land, a sabbath to the Lord;* you shall not sow your field or prune your vineyard" (Leviticus 25: 3, 4, emphasis added). This "sabbath of the land" (verse 6) allowed for its rejuvenation.

God was serious. The violation of the sabbatical land rest came under the covenant curses/judgments. God vowed: "I will scatter you among the nations. . . . Then the land shall rest, and enjoy its sabbaths" (Leviticus 26:33-35).

Thus, the chronicler recorded that the Babylonian overthrow of

Judah brought about the fulfillment of "the word of the Lord by the mouth of Jeremiah, until the land had enjoyed its sabbaths. All the days that it lay desolate it kept sabbath, to fulfil seventy years" (2 Chronicles 36:21). Since the Babylonians never repopulated the territory of Judah with other peoples (as was the practice of the Assyrians—see 2 Kings 17:24), the tillable lands of Judah lay fallow. Ten sabbatical units of years contributed to its revitalization.

Twice the Lord compared the future "exodus" from Babylon with the exodus from Egypt (see Jeremiah 16:14, 15; 23:7, 8). The linking of these two lands—Egypt and Babylonia—implies in this context that it takes considerable time to process a people into a nation. In Egypt, Jacob's clan grew into a nation numbered by the hundreds of thousands (see Exodus 12:37). In Babylon the physical increase was evidently not as great. But time was needed to transform an idolatrous, discouraged, and demoralized people into a new Israel— an Israel with a new spiritual commitment to God and a strong covenant relationship with Him. The generation of apostates would need to die out.

God protected Jacob's family in Egypt from pagan influence by causing the clan to settle in Goshen, separate to some degree from the masses of the Egyptians. Probably the stigma of being a conquered and captive people, looked down on and ridiculed by their conquerors (see Psalm 137:1-4), kept the Judaists segregated from the Babylonians. Even after many years at the Babylonian court, Daniel was still sneeringly identified by King Belshazzar as "one of the exiles of Judah" (Daniel 5:13), and his Persian associates likewise employed the expression when they accused him to King Darius (see Daniel 6:13).

The synagogue system developed during the Babylonian captivity. Tradition attributes the institution's founding to the prophet Ezekiel. The synagogue functioned as the center of Jewish life— school, worship, court. Here the Scriptures (what was then available) became the focus of study and kept the light of faith burning in the hearts of the new, oncoming generations. The ministry of Ezekiel and the synagogue-centers both had their part in preserving a remnant of faith for the future and the coming of the Messiah.

Having announced to Judah that the nation would undergo a seventy-year discipline by the power of Babylon, God immediately noted that Babylon herself would come under judgment. *"After seventy years are completed,* I will punish the king of Babylon and that nation, the land of the Chaldeans, for their iniquity, says the Lord, making the land an everlasting waste" (Jeremiah 25:12, emphasis added).

When the Babylonian Empire finally toppled with the taking of the city of Babylon by Cyrus and his Median-Persian forces in 539 B.C., Daniel excitedly turned to the study of Jeremiah's prophecies (particularly, our chapters 25 and 29) and those in Isaiah (chapters 44 and 45). These foretold the length of the captivity and the release to be granted by the conquering Cyrus (see Daniel 9:2, 3).

Human accountability

As Creator, God holds all people and nations accountable to Him. Although sin has marred His image within humankind, yet the general principles couched in the second table of the Ten Commandments (defining human obligation) seem known to some degree in every place. Just as the Spirit moved "over the face of the waters" (Genesis 1:2), we have reason to believe that He moves upon the great seas of humankind (sometimes symbolized by moving waters—Revelation 17:15), illuminating the Creator's will to them. Accountability to spiritual light—much or little—is always a serious matter, and God "has fixed a day on which he will judge the world in righteousness" (Acts 17:31). But He also acts at times to restrain the tide of evil.

"Take from my hand this cup of the wine of wrath," God commanded Jeremiah in vision, shortly after announcing the seventy-year captivity. "Make all the nations to whom I send you drink it. They shall drink and stagger and be crazed because of the sword which I am sending among them" (Jeremiah 25:15, 16). With this commission, Jeremiah entered in on his assignment as a prophet to non-Jewish nations as well as to Judah (see Jeremiah 1:9, 10).

The action of presenting the cup to the nations, of course, is figurative, although the prophet did send an oral message to several nations by their envoys on one occasion (see Jeremiah 27:1-11). It is also possible that the written prophecies against the nations (chapters 46 to 49) were sent to their respective states. But the prophecy that foretold the overthrow of the Babylonian Empire (chapters 50 and 51) was ceremonially buried in the Euphrates River (see Jeremiah 51:59-64).

Literally, the Hebrew reads, "the cup of wine, this wrath" (Jeremiah 25:15). The symbol is common to both Testaments of the

Bible.[4] God's "wrath" is not like human anger, but is the divine judgment on sin. To "drink" His wrath is to receive His just judgment or punishment for transgression.

The list of nations that would come under God's judgment at this time (see Jeremiah 25:15-26) begins with Jerusalem/Judah and ends, surprisingly, with Babylon itself.[5] The nations to which specific prophecies are addressed in chapters 46-51 are included in this longer list in chapter 25 (except for Damascus/Syria)—more than a score of nations. It is evident that the sweep of names is intended to portray the entire Near East as coming under divine judgment at this time. God explains why: "Thus says the Lord of hosts [to the nations of the Near East]: You must drink! For behold, I begin to work evil at the city which is called by my name [Jerusalem], and shall you go unpunished? You shall not go unpunished, for I am summoning a sword against all the inhabitants of the earth, says the Lord of hosts" (Jeremiah 25:28, 29). Judah was highly accountable because of her greater understanding of God's will and her refusal to obey Him. But the surrounding nations—with less light—were equally accountable for their refusal to live and govern their peoples according to what they knew was morally right.

Judgment on Babylon

It is only natural that we should wonder at God's method of using the Babylonian conquest as the means to discipline the Near Eastern nations—including Judah—and then, later on, to discipline Babylon by some of these same nations it had conquered (such as Media—Jeremiah 51:11, 28; see also Isaiah 13:17). Here is a biblical philosophy of history that is worthy of our study.

God designed that human society should be orderly and governed (see Romans 13:1-7). And this governing of society is to be according to moral principles as expressed in the second table of the Ten Commandments. In the dream God gave Nebuchadnezzar regarding his future, He depicted the true purpose of government in the form of a great tree with fruitful, wide-spreading branches. The tree provided food for all, shelter for the birds, and shade and protection to the animals gathered under its boughs (see Daniel 4:10-12). "This representation shows the character of a government that fulfills God's purpose—a government that protects and upbuilds the nation."[6]

God permits nations to come upon the stage of the world theater, as it were. If they govern their peoples in harmony with the moral principles embedded in His creation, they prosper, and their peoples are happy. But if, in their governance, they become oppressive and cruel, violating these fundamental moral principles, it is only a matter of time before such governments fail, and their glory fades. Human history is replete with examples of political states whose arrogance and oppression exited them into oblivion.

As the superpower in the Near East, the Babylonian Empire might have ruled as protector of the diverse peoples that populated the Fertile Crescent—might have contributed to their prosperity, functioning as the symbolic tree in Nebuchadnezzar's dream (see Daniel 4). But as the nation enlarged its borders and increased in wealth, political sagacity, and military prowess, it became proud and arrogant. Greed marked the course of its rise to supremacy.

No non-Jewish nation in antiquity received greater and more direct attention by God than did Babylon. The witness of Daniel and his companions—in the school and in the service of the court and state—greatly impressed Nebuchadnezzar. Daniel's interpretation of the king's dream (see Daniel 2), as well as the king's insanity and recovery (see Daniel 4), led Nebuchadnezzar to acknowledge the true God time after time. But the subsequent rulers did not profit by Nebuchadnezzar's experience. "We would have healed Babylon," the Lord declared, "but she was not healed" (Jeremiah 51:9).

As a nation, Babylon clung to its idols. The height of its blasphemy came when Belshazzar and his thousand lords and his wives and concubines drank from the gold and silver vessels taken from God's temple and praised their gods of metal, wood, and stone for Babylon's apparent victory over the Creator of the heaven and earth (see Daniel 5:1-4)!

Although the fate of Babylon lay far in the future, Jeremiah wrote down the judgments that God had spelled out against the nation (largely in our chapters 50 and 51). He instructed Seraiah, an official in Zedekiah's court and a brother to his secretary Baruch, to take this scroll of judgment along when he accompanied Zedekiah on the latter's trip to Babylon in 593 B.C. to render his loyalty oath to Nebuchadnezzar (see Jeremiah 51:59). On the banks of the Euphrates, Saraiah was to read the scroll—probably aloud—tie it to a stone, and hurl it into the river as he cried out: "Thus shall Babylon sink, to rise no more, because of the evil that I am bringing upon her" (Jeremiah 51:64).

Thus, the punishment of Judah, her Near Eastern neighbors, and Babylon itself portrays the even-handed discipline and justice of earth's divine Sovereign.

The day of the Lord

The symbolic act of causing sinful nations to drink the wine cup of God's "wrath"—His judgment on sin—is more regularly described in the Bible by the expression "the day of the Lord." The latter expression implies that humanity—socially organized in city-states, nations, and other political units—has its "day," its opportunity to flourish, as we have observed above. However, should their violations of the principles of righteousness exceed His boundaries, God intervenes, either directly (the Flood; the destruction of Sodom and Gomorrah) or indirectly (permitting other nations to redress the situation). This intervention is denoted as "the day of the Lord"—His day, His time.

Thus, the "day of the Lord" is a day of judgment, a day of destruction to evildoers, a kind of "close of probation" of that particular city or nation. At the same time, it may also be a day of deliverance for God's true people.[7] The conquest of the Babylonian Empire by the Medes and Persians, described by Jeremiah (see Jeremiah 50, 51), is called the "day of the Lord" by Isaiah (see Isaiah 13:1, 6, 17). And the overthrow of Judah by the Babylonians, which Jeremiah also describes (see Jeremiah 4:6, 7, 19-31), is likewise referred to as the "day of the Lord" by Zephaniah and Joel (see Zephaniah 1:1, 14-18; Joel 1:15).

Strikingly, these "local" judgments are often expressed in cosmic terms! For example, Micah announces the day of the Lord on Israel and Judah (see Micah 1:1, 3) in terms of the mountains melting "like wax before the fire" (verse 4). Isaiah depicts the day of the Lord on Babylon as accompanied by a darkening of the sun, moon, and stars (see Isaiah 13:1, 6, 10). Jeremiah's description of the day of the Lord on Judah, however, is possibly the most graphic in the entire Old Testament:

> I looked on the earth, and lo, it was *waste and void* [the same phrase in Hebrew is also used to describe the original chaos—Genesis 1:2]; and to the heavens, and they had no light. I looked on the mountains, and lo, they were quaking. . . . I looked, and lo, there was no man, and all the birds of the

air had fled. I looked, and lo, the fruitful land was a desert, and all its cities were laid in ruins before the Lord, before his fierce anger (Jeremiah 4:23-26, emphasis added).

How is such language to be understood? The capture of Babylon and the downfall of that empire in 539 B.C. didn't darken the celestial lights, nor did the mountains melt and the earth return to its primeval chaos when Judah was overrun in 586 B.C. Some dismiss the cosmic language as poetic hyperbole. But the New Testament portrayal of the "day of the Lord" as the second coming of Christ depicts similar cosmic phenomena as literally occurring. For example, the apostle Peter writes of Christ's return in this manner:

The day of the Lord will come like a thief, and then *the heavens will pass away with a loud noise, and the elements will be dissolved* with fire, and the earth and the works that are upon it will be burned up (2 Peter 3:10, emphasis added).

The revelator adds that a gigantic earthquake will convulse the earth, causing mountains and islands to disappear while giant hailstones pound the earth to rubble (see Revelation 16:17-21).

In view of the New Testament's testimony (and other texts could be added), it is evident that the "day of the Lord" passages in the Old Testament have a double focus. The prophets are shown the ultimate Day of the Lord (Christ's second coming and executive judgment) at the same time they are shown the local "day of the Lord" on their particular situation. For us, it means that every "local," historical "day of the Lord" is a lesson book of what is yet to come in the final "Day." For the Judaists in Jeremiah's time, the "day of the Lord" on Judah meant the judgment and ruin of the nation under the "hammer" blows of Babylon (see Jeremiah 50:23).

Would Judah attempt to escape its relentless enemy like Jezebel, who sought to divert Jehu's sword by her charm and cosmetics? (see 2 Kings 9:30). Jeremiah challenged the nation: "You, O desolate one, what do you mean that you dress in scarlet, that you deck yourself with ornaments of gold, that you enlarge your eyes with paint? In vain you beautify yourself. Your lovers despise you; they seek your life" (Jeremiah 4:30).

Not the external riches of the land, nor its prosperity, nor its military might could prevent the wheels of the Chaldean war chariot from crushing out the national life. This was the "day of the Lord." Judah was rotten at its core. Only a spiritually revived and internally renewed people, clothed in the Lord's righteousness, could expect divine deliverance.

---

1. Jeremiah may be referring to Huldah (see 2 Kings 22:3-20), Zephaniah (see Zephaniah 1:1), and Uriah (see Jeremiah 26:20-23), and possibly others, whose names were never recorded. Habakkuk and Joel are listed by some scholars as ministering around 630 and 620 B.C., respectively.

2. This passage (Jeremiah 25:8-10) contains a common Hebraic thought pattern we have noted elsewhere: In the Bible—especially in the Old Testament—God is often said to do things that He permits or doesn't prevent. God did not *personally* "send" for all the tribes of the north or for Nebuchadnezzar to conquer these lands. The Lord simply withdrew His restraints. Nor did He prevent Nebuchadnezzar from expanding his selfish conquests. Although the Hebrews understood secondary causes, they normally spoke in terms of attributing all happenings in the earth to the Creator, the Sovereign Lord.

3. The Hebrew noun *'ōlām*, translated here as "everlasting" (Jeremiah 25:9 [RSV], "perpetual" [KJV]), and with the Greek adjective *aiōnios*, "eternal/everlasting" (Septuagint/LXX) does not denote "endlessness" in itself. Its emphasis is upon unbroken duration and not upon the length of an action. The length is determined by the nature of the subject so described. Thus, it is clear that "everlasting/perpetual" in this instance means an unbroken period of seventy years and not an "endless" condition. The reproach of the captivity would last for seventy years. It would be removed at the end of that time by the amazing favor of several Persian kings, who would decree Judah's release from exile, the rebuilding of the temple at state expense, and the restoration of the Jewish nation as a political entity.

4. See Isaiah 51:17, 22; Psalm 75:8; Revelation 14:9, 10, etc. Although Jesus was personally sinless, He drank the cup of God's wrath/judgment on sin (see Luke 22:42) because the sins of the world were imputed to Him as our Sin Bearer (see 2 Corinthians 5:21; 1 Peter 2:24).

5. "Babylon" (Jeremiah 25:26, RSV) is given as the English equivalent to the Hebrew *sheshak* in the text (transliterated as *Sheshach* in the KJV and margin of the RSV). It appears that the usual Hebrew word for Babylon (*babel*) is written in this verse according to a code of writing known as *Atbash*. In this cipher the first letter is substituted for the last letter in the Hebrew alphabet, the second for the next-to-the-last, and so on. Thus, the Hebrew *beth* (b), the second letter of the Hebrew alphabet was substituted with the *shin* (sh), the next to the last letter (thus: b, b = sh, sh), and the *lamed* (l) for the *kaph* (k). Thus, with a slight change in the vowels, *babel* (=Babylon) in the code (= sh-sh-k) became *sheshak*. (Note that the Hebrew alphabet contains only consonants. Also, some transliterate the *kaph* (k) with (ch) rather than a (k); hence the word: *Sheshach*.

6. Ellen G. White, *Education* (Boise, Idaho: Pacific Press Publishing Association, 1952), 175.

7. See *SDABC*, vol. 4, comment on Isaiah 13:6, for a useful discussion of the expression "the day of the Lord."

Chapter 10

Prophets of Peace

From the beginning, the participants in the Philadelphia Convention (1787) agreed that there should be three powers of government—legislative, executive, and judicial—and that these should be separate, as far as possible. In this manner the Congress (legislative) would act as a check on the presidency (executive), and the latter would balance the former. The judiciary would function as a check on both the president and Congress. Thus, the Constitution of the United States came to embody a series of checks and balances between the three branches of government that have provided for the successful administration of the federal government of the United States of America.

Three powers also controlled the governing of Israel during the monarchical period. The Mosaic legislation established a theocracy (a union of "church and state") in which God ruled His people directly through leaders like Moses and Joshua and, eventually (in theory, at least), through the Davidic dynasty. God's laws—moral, civil, and ritual—provided the "Constitution" of the nation and were enforced by the powers of the royal court and temple. Over against the king and priest stood the prophet, whom God raised up from time to time with messages of encouragement or reproof that might be addressed to persons in either office. The prophet was not actually an officer of government, but he or she often had a strong impact on the royal policy.

This trio of powers—designated as "the shepherds who care for my people" (Jeremiah 23:2)—naturally influenced the morality and prosperity of the nation, the lesser officials taking their cue from the higher powers. The *spiritual* quality of the nation was largely determined by these ruling entities, especially the kingship.

A dominant king might manipulate the priesthood to his own ends, and sometimes the priesthood and the king were in corrupt accord. This the people could see. But a more serious situation developed when "false" prophets began *to endorse* the wrongs of both court and temple with a "Thus says the Lord"! Then, both prince and priest might be deceived, as well as the people.

Characteristics of false prophets

A so-called false prophet is really not a prophet at all. His ministry is a sham, a pretense. When Jeremiah talked over the matter with God, he noted the tremendous influence the false prophets were having on the people. The Lord replied: "The prophets are prophesying lies in my name; I did not send them. . . . They are prophesying to you a lying vision, worthless divination, and the deceit of their own minds" (Jeremiah 14:14).

God also informed Jeremiah, "The prophets prophesied by Baal, and went after things that do not profit" (Jeremiah 2:8). As "broad-minded" men of their times, they apparently attempted to accommodate the worship of Baal and the other gods to the religion of Yahweh, but the resultant hybrid was unacceptable. In every generation some men and women within the church try to commingle current religious beliefs and practices to the true faith as revealed in the Scriptures. Jeremiah's generation was no different.

The false prophets and priests condemned no sins and made no appeals to the people to repent of their godless lives. They had abdicated their role as spiritual leaders and were bent on winning financial gain, regardless of how it was obtained. "From the least to the greatest every one is greedy for unjust gain; from prophet to priest every one deals falsely," the Lord told Jeremiah (Jeremiah 8:10; see also chapter 6:13).

The spiritual leaders participated with the people in the same evils. "Both prophet and priest are ungodly; even in my house I have found their wickedness," the Lord said (Jeremiah 23:11). Consternation gripped Jeremiah as he came to understand why the false prophets had neither inclination nor influence to lift the people spiritually (see verse 9). "In the prophets of Jerusalem I have seen a horrible thing: they commit adultery and walk in lies; they strengthen the hands of evildoers, so that no one turns from his wickedness" (verse 14). They corrupted the nation's morals.

Peace movement

A priest by accident of birth (house of Aaron) and a prophet by calling, it was only natural that Jeremiah clashed with these two groups of religious leaders more than with the kings who ruled during the last decades of Judah's statehood. Josiah's reading from "the book of the law" led him, as king, to realize that divine judgment threatened the nation. And the prophetess Huldah confirmed his fears (see 2 Kings 22:15-17). Jeremiah and his associates (such as Zephaniah) were prompted by God's Spirit to give similar warnings.

But the false prophets countered these warnings, even in the days of Josiah. "They [the "prophets" and priests] have healed the wound of my people lightly, saying, 'Peace, peace,' when there is no peace," said God (Jeremiah 6:14; 8:11). Thus began a "peace movement" in Judah that seemed to gather momentum in spite of Josiah's death (608 B.C.) and the two successful invasions and deportations by the Babylonians that rapidly followed (605, 597 B.C.).

The "peace movement" made Jeremiah's task seemingly insuperable. To the perplexed people, it was the word of one prophet against the word of another, since both Jeremiah and the false prophets claimed to speak in the name of the Lord. "Ah, Lord God," Jeremiah prayed, "behold, the prophets say to them, 'You shall not see the sword, nor shall you have famine, but I will give you assured peace in this place' " (Jeremiah 14:13).

In an endeavor to break this prophetic "gridlock," God sent Jeremiah back to the people with a specific message on this question: Who really spoke for God? "Thus says the Lord of hosts: 'Do not listen to the words of the prophets who prophesy to you, filling you with vain hopes; they speak visions of their own minds, not from the mouth of the Lord' " (Jeremiah 23:16)

God targeted their audiences—the kinds of persons to whom the "prophets" promised peace—implying that this fact alone should have opened the eyes of the people to the true source of their allegedly inspired oracles: "They say continually *to those who despise the word of the Lord*, 'It shall be well with you'; and *to every one who stubbornly follows his own heart*, they say, 'No evil shall come upon you' " (verse 17, emphasis added).

Although these "prophets" received no vision from God, we must not think that they had nothing of substance to say or that their reasoning did not appear convincing to the kings and princes, as well as to the populace. And what they had to say was welcome news.

As observed earlier, the "temple theology" of the priests was persuasive. God, they affirmed "with chapter and verse," had indeed promised permanence to the Davidic dynasty, Jerusalem, and the temple. It would be inconceivable for Him to bring about the overthrow of this triad of special institutions. The "prophets" also developed their own line of reasoning.

As time passed, the "prophets" thought they could see cracks developing in the supposed "invincible" empire. Babylon was vulnerable; twice in the past a strong Egyptian army had halted the Chaldean war machine for a time (608, 601 B.C.). And now, Egypt, under Psamtik II, was building up its forces and consolidating its gains (593, 592 B.C.). Insurrection had broken out in the eastern part of the empire—involving even elements of the army (595, 594 B.C.). Nebuchadnezzar's call for a loyalty oath before the golden image on the Plain of Dura could be perceived as a sign of weakness, rather than strength—an attempt to prevent a general uprising in all parts of the empire by browbeating his subject rulers (594/593 B.C.).

The "prophets" undoubtedly reasoned that if the national forces in the western part of the empire—together with the support of a strong Egypt—were to pool their resources, the overthrow of Babylon would be certain. Then, when the clash of arms sounded, other subject nations would join the breakaway as well. All the political weather vanes pointed to clearing skies! Before long, Judah would be free from the Babylonian threat Jeremiah kept harping about.

Such reasoning was irresistible and had such an influence over Zedekiah that Jeremiah pleaded with him personally: "Do not listen to the words of the prophets who are saying to you, 'You shall not serve the king of Babylon,' for it is a lie which they are prophesying to you. I have not sent them, says the Lord, but they are prophesying falsely in my name, with the result that I will drive you out and you will perish, you and the prophets who are prophesying to you" (Jeremiah 27:14, 15).

Jeremiah records no response from the king. He turned to the priests, who were likewise being deceived. "Don't listen to the prophets who are saying that the temple vessels taken by Nebuchadnezzar will be brought back shortly," he urged. "It is a lie." And then he challenged: "If they are prophets . . . let them intercede with the Lord of hosts, that the vessels which are left . . . may not go to Babylon" (verses 16-18). But, he added sadly, "they shall be carried to Babylon" (verse 22). Jeremiah's pleas were useless.

Confrontation with Hananiah

But how could it be determined which prophets were speaking God's true "end-time" message? An examination of "the book of the law"—the Mosaic writings—would have disclosed whose message was in harmony with God's previously spoken word. But it is not likely that the masses had access to it or to the writings of the other pre-exilic prophets. The practice of publicly reading Deuteronomy to the people in the sabbatical year at the time of the Feast of Tabernacles had probably ceased (see Deuteronomy 31:10, 11).

Be that as it may, the strength of the ever-growing peace movement in Jerusalem finally prompted Hananiah, one of the false prophets, to confront Jeremiah face to face in the main court of the temple in the presence of both priests and people.

According to the chapter's dateline (see Jeremiah 28:1), the public challenge took place in the fifth month of Zedekiah's fourth year, our July/August, 593 B.C. Perhaps the recent revolt in Babylonia (December 595 B.C.–January 594 B.C.) was the political straw in the wind that motivated Hananiah to make his daring proclamation. It may also have been related to the plotting of the ambassadors from the surrounding nations who had assembled at Zedekiah's court about this same time (see Jeremiah 27:2, 3).

"Thus says the Lord of hosts, the God of Israel," Hananiah trumpeted in the temple court. "I have broken the yoke of the king of Babylon. Within two years I will bring back to this place all the vessels of the Lord's house. . . . I will also bring back to this place Jeconiah [Jehoiachin] . . . , king of Judah, and all the exiles from Judah who went to Babylon, . . . for I will break the yoke of the king of Babylon" (Jeremiah 28:2-4).

Hananiah's declaration was not wishful thinking, to which he deceptively added God's endorsement. Rather, he intended to contradict Jeremiah's plain prediction that King Jehoiachin would "not return" to Judah (see Jeremiah 22:24-27) and that the captivity would involve an extended period of seventy years (see Jeremiah 29:1-4, 10). Hananiah disputed the predictions that Jeremiah spoke at God's command (see Jeremiah 28:4).

The wide-sweeping announcement immediately caused the people to look at Jeremiah. Both men claimed to speak in the name of the Lord, but the messages were contradictory. Who really did speak for Yahweh? How would Jeremiah respond to this calling of his hand? However, Jeremiah gave no hint that this sudden attack on his veracity disturbed him. He had probably pondered many times before just how true and false prophets could be distinguished.

"Amen!" the startled throng heard him thunder! "So be it!" "May the Lord make the words which you have prophesied come true" (Jeremiah 28:6). Then Jeremiah began to reason something like this:

But, Hananiah, you lack a perspective that must not be omitted: the prophets who preceded you and me "prophesied [that] war, famine, and pestilence" were coming. *That has been my message too.* Now, you say that peace is about to come. So your message is not only out of harmony with mine, but also with those of the previous prophets. There is only one way left to determine whose message is correct—if you don't accept the work of the earlier prophets as endorsing my message: "The prophet who prophesies peace, when the word of that prophet comes to pass, then it will be known that the Lord has truly sent the prophet" (see Jeremiah 28:7-9; see also Deuteronomy 18:20-22).

Jeremiah had answered well. Neither Hananiah, the priests, or the people could deny that earlier prophets, such as Micah (see Jeremiah 26:18), Isaiah (see Isaiah 1:18-25), and others as far back as Amos (see Amos 2:4, 5), had predicted doom on Jerusalem and Judah. Jeremiah's messages were in harmony with these acknowledged prophets.

But Hananiah cleverly sidestepped a reply to Jeremiah. He substituted dramatic action instead. Stepping forward, he lifted the yoke from Jeremiah's neck and broke it, flinging the pieces to the ground as he shouted, "Thus says the Lord: Even so will I break the yoke of Nebuchadnezzar king of Babylon from the neck of all the nations within two years" (Jeremiah 28:11).

As the people watched, Jeremiah silently walked away. He had appealed to the best authority for the validation of his messages— the writings of the earlier prophets. Only time could prove who was right. He did not know, of course, that within five years Nebuchadnezzar would begin the final siege of Jerusalem, and Judah would be overrun with Chaldean troops.

But God didn't wait five years to vindicate His servant. He sent

Jeremiah back to Hananiah with a message. We may suppose that this second confrontation took place before the same crowds in the temple court. Because of Hananiah's bold insubordination, God said that He would impose "an iron yoke of servitude to Nebuchadnezzar" on Judah and the surrounding nations (verse 14).

Then, looking the pretender straight in the eye, Jeremiah said: "Listen, Hananiah, the Lord has not sent you, and you have made this people trust in a lie. Therefore . . . *'this very year you shall die, because you have uttered rebellion against the Lord'*" (verses 15, 16, emphasis added). Two months later Hananiah lay dead (verses 1, 17). God strikingly affirmed His servant, but there is no record that the defiant attitudes of the "prophets," priests, or princes softened.

Problem prophets in the exile

Shortly after the deportation of 597 B.C., Jeremiah wrote a letter to advise the exiles on how to relate to their captivity. Several false prophets were among them, and like Hananiah, they kept the people in an unhealthy state of excitement and unrest with false hopes of their soon release.

"Do not let your prophets and your diviners who are among you deceive you . . . for it is a lie which they are prophesying to you" in the Lord's name, Jeremiah penned (Jeremiah 29:8, 9). Unrest among the exiles would provoke harsh, oppressive measures by the authorities; unnecessary restrictions would then be imposed on the Jews. The captivity would be long, and they should make every effort to adjust to it and live as normally as possible (verses 4-10).

The exiles had rejoiced to find "prophets" among them ("You have said, 'The Lord has raised up prophets for us in Babylon' "—verse 15). These men fomented rebellion among the captives. Look, they may have argued, Judah's throne, temple, capital, and country are still intact! That is because we are going back any day now! But once more, Jeremiah repeated the unwelcomed message from God: sword, famine, and pestilence were about to decimate Judah; the kingdom was tottering (verses 15-19).

Moreover, Jeremiah had a word from the Lord in regard to Ahab and Zedekiah, two false prophets who were at the center of the agitation. Nebuchadnezzar would summarily execute them, Jeremiah predicted. So swift and shocking would be their deaths that a curse would come into popular use among them: "The Lord make you like Zedekiah and Ahab, whom the king of Babylon roasted in the fire" (verse 22).[1]

In addition, Jeremiah exposed their corrupt private lives. The captives may have expressed their doubt, because the Lord directed His servant to add His personal statement, as it were, to the letter: "I am the one who knows, and I am witness, says the Lord" (verse 23; see also Hebrews 4:13).

Shemaiah, another of the false prophets in the exile, fought back. He endeavored to secure the support of the priests and populace in Jerusalem by writing an open letter to each. A third letter he sent to Zephaniah, the second-ranking priest (see Jeremiah 52:24). Zephaniah took no action, but simply read Shemaiah's letter to Jeremiah.

In the document Shemaiah angrily asks why Zephaniah has not rebuked this "madman" and locked him "in the stocks and collar"? (Jeremiah 29:25-29). God directed Jeremiah to reply with an open letter himself to the exiles with regard to Shemaiah. Because he, too, "prophesied" the lie of peace and a short exile, neither he nor his descendants would live to participate in the restoration of Judah (verses 31, 32). Shemaiah and his family would die; not a single descendant would live to see the "homeland."

Messengers without a message

It is an awesome position for any human to stand between the Creator and a judgment-bound people as His spokesman. As the apostolic writer says, "One does not take the honor upon himself, but he is called of God" (Hebrews 5:4). Yet the false prophet, without divine authorization and without a message from God, audaciously dares to speak for Him. "I did not send the prophets, yet they ran," God said. "I did not speak to them, yet they prophesied" (Jeremiah 23:21). And multiplied thousands believed their lies and perished! How are we in modern times to discern between true and false representatives of God? Jeremiah's reply to Hananiah provides one important key: The true prophet/teacher will speak in harmony with the previous revelations of earlier true prophets (see Jeremiah 28:7, 8). God supplies another key: The true prophet entreats the people to turn "from their evil way, and from the evil of their doings" (Jeremiah 23:22).

The omnipotent, omniscient God is fully acquainted with what is occurring on earth. No one can hide from Him (verses 23, 24). He hears what the false prophets say, as they claim His authority. But their teachings are only "straw." The Lord appeals to the true teacher of His Word: "Let him who has my word speak my word faithfully. What has straw in common with wheat? says the Lord. Is not my word like fire, says the Lord, and like a hammer which breaks the rock in pieces?" (verses 28, 29).

The true messenger never lulls the sinner into complacency with sweet words that all is well. " 'There is no peace,' says the Lord, 'for the wicked' " (Isaiah 48:22). The true presentation of God's word acts like a cleansing fire to burn away sin (see Isaiah 6:6, 7) and like a hammer that smashes the stony heart, rendering it broken in repentance and contrition (see Psalm 51:17).

On this side of the cross, Christians have two tests—in addition to the two mentioned by Jeremiah—by which to critique the claims of an alleged prophet/teacher. Jesus gave us one of these: "Beware of false prophets, who come to you in sheep's clothing but inwardly are ravenous wolves. You will know them by their fruits. . . . A sound tree cannot bear evil fruit, nor can a bad tree bear good fruit. . . . Thus you will know them by their fruits" (Matthew 7:15-20). These fruits will be seen in the influence of the claimant's life and teachings. A period of maturation is necessary, but ultimately, good will never issue from a corrupt heart or message.

Near the close of his life, John was inspired by the Spirit to lay out one more important instrument for testing. He wrote: "Test the spirits to see whether they are of God; for many false prophets have gone out into the world. By this you know the Spirit of God: every spirit which confesses that Jesus Christ has come in the flesh is of God" (1 John 4:1, 2).

This counsel may be summed up as a test of loyalty to Jesus Christ. It not only means that the claimant believes in the incarnation of Christ, but it also implies that he believes in His full Deity, in His preexistence before His virgin birth, in the biblically stated facts and purpose for His sinless life, His bodily resurrection and ascension, His priesthood, and His second coming in glory and majesty to complete the plan of salvation.

With these guidelines supplied by God through Jeremiah, John, and the Lord Jesus Himself, the Christian need not be led astray by the false teachers who cry "peace and safety" in our modern age (see 1 Thessalonians 5:1-11) or who offer any other deception.

---

1. The Babylonians used burning as a form of capital punishment (see Daniel 3:6).

Chapter 11

Precious Promises

"When hope is alive, the night is less dark; the solitude less deep, fear less acute," says an anonymous writer.[1] Less picturesque, but more practical, are the words of the apostle Paul: "If we hope for what we do not see, we wait for it with patience" (Romans 8:25). A living hope galvanizes the fainting spirit and arouses a determination to persevere.

For that reason God instructed Jeremiah to write in a scroll His plans for the future of His people. These written promises would be an important instrument to offset the depression and demoralization that would inevitably settle into the Jewish community when all the exiles of the several deportations eventually mixed together in foreign lands.

> Write in a book all the words that I have spoken to you. For behold, days are coming, . . . when I will restore the fortunes of my people, Israel and Judah, says the Lord, and I will bring them back to the land which I gave to their fathers, and they shall take possession of it (Jeremiah 30:2, 3).

Scholars generally delimit this scroll (referred to as "The Book of Consolation") to chapters 30 and 31. Others would include chapters 32 and 33 as well. This is a minor point. The compiler probably placed these four chapters together because all four deal with the restoration to Palestine after the discipline of captivity.

The subjects of these chapters form the climax to Jeremiah's writings. Like a magnifying glass, gathering the rays of the sun to focus with intense heat on a single point, so this collection of oracles concentrates on the future beyond the captivity—a future that included not only the restoration from Babylon but also the advent of the Messiah Himself and the age to follow.

Heading the list of promises is God's affirmation that the breach between Judah and Israel would be closed. They would return as *one* people (see Jeremiah 30:3, 4; 3:18; Ezekiel 37:15-28).

The descendants of these former kingdoms would return with chastened hearts and a spirit of contrition, fully determined to enter a committed covenant relationship with God. "The people of Israel and the people of Judah shall come together, weeping as they come; and they shall seek the Lord their God. They shall ask the way to Zion, with faces turned toward it, saying, 'Come, let us join ourselves to the Lord in an everlasting covenant which will never be forgotten' " (Jeremiah 50:4, 5).

Jacob and Rachel

The "Book of Consolations" has, at first, a bittersweet taste. Since it concerns "Israel and Judah" (Jeremiah 30:4), it is natural for the Lord to recall the names of Jacob and Rachel, whom we may view, in this instance, as the cofounders of the united nation. It may be objected that Leah and the two concubines bore ten of the progenitors, while Rachel personally bore only Joseph and Benjamin.

However, Jacob "adopted" Joseph's two sons, Manasseh and Ephraim, into his immediate family (see Genesis 48:5). And the tribe of Ephraim became so large and dominant that its name is often used interchangeably with "Israel" to denote the entire nation of the northern kingdom of ten tribes (see Hosea 4:16, 17; 7:1; 11:1-3; 14:1, 8, etc.). In Jeremiah 30 and 31, Jacob's name is linked to Judah and Rachel's to both nations', but especially to Ephraim/Israel. The prophecy begins by portraying "Jacob" writhing in agony (30:5-7):

Thus says the Lord: We have heard a cry of panic, of terror, and no peace. Ask now, and see, can a man bear a child? Why then do I see every man with his hands on his loins like a woman in labor? Why has every face turned pale? Alas! that day is so great there is none like it; it is a time of distress for Jacob; yet he shall be saved out of it.

Jeremiah employs the figure of "a woman in hard labor" in six other passages as well. Four times the symbol is used in connection with the conquest of Judah by Babylon (see Jeremiah 4:31; 6:24; 13:21; 22:23); once in the setting of the conquest of Damascus/Syria by the same power (see Jeremiah 49:24); and once in terms of Babylon's own collapse (see Jeremiah 50:43).

Allusions by Bible writers to a woman's birth pangs usually emphasize one or both of two aspects: their sudden onset or their excruciating and exhausting pain. In this passage the Lord is again underscoring the terrible experience Judah would undergo in Babylon's final invasion, siege, and conquest. The suffering would be intense; it would seem like "every man" was in the throes of labor. "Jacob" personifies the whole nation; and in its primary setting, this "time of distress for Jacob" ("the time of Jacob's trouble," KJV) describes the agony of the sixth-century-B.C. destruction and exile of Judah. But the promise is made: "*He* [Jacob, representing Judah] *shall be saved out of it*" (Jeremiah 30:7, emphasis added).[2]

The Lord's reference to Rachel is recorded in chapter 31:15-17. "Thus says the Lord: 'A voice is heard in Ramah, lamentation and bitter weeping. Rachel is weeping for her children; she refuses to be comforted for her children, because they are not'" (verse 15).

The birthing figure of "hard labor" is the underlying matrix that ties these symbols of Jacob and Rachel together in the Jeremiah prophecy. After visiting Bethel for a second time (see Genesis 35:1), Jacob turned south to continue his return journey from Syria to Isaac's home in Hebron. Rachel was pregnant with her second child. As they journeyed from Bethel to Ephrath (Bethlehem), a distance of about twelve miles (Jerusalem lies between, nearly on a direct line), Rachel went into labor. Twice it is said that she had "hard labor" (verses 16, 17). The struggle exhausted her life forces, and although she gave birth to a son, named through her pain and tears "Benoni" ("son of my sorrow"), she died.

Jacob buried Rachel "on the way" to the town later known as Bethlehem and marked the grave with a stone (see verses 18-20). Consequently, in later years her grave came to be associated with Bethlehem (south of Jerusalem). But according to other data, Rachel was buried north of Jerusalem, near the border town of Ramah in the territory of the tribe of Benjamin (see Joshua 18: 21, 25), where the latter juxtaposes with the territory of Ephraim (see 1 Samuel 10:2; Jeremiah 31:15), a gravesite still between Bethel and Bethlehem.

The Babylonians assembled the Jewish captives in chains at

Ramah to organize them for the overland trek to Mesopotamia and exile (see Jeremiah 40:1). We can scarcely imagine the weeping and moaning of this mass of broken humanity—weakened by famine and disease, traumatized by the loss of loved ones, homes, temple, city, and nation, and dreading the forced march that would leave thousands more dead by the roadside!

Little wonder that the Lord recalls the bitter weeping of their ancestor Rachel and hears in her birthing screams the bitter weeping and lamentations of the Judaists encamped near her grave as they await an unknown future. It is as though the "motherland" were weeping for her lost populations—both by the sword and deportation. But "Rachel" is (like "Jacob") a large, inclusive symbol, embracing the whole house of Israel. She weeps for the departing Judaists (composed of the people of Benjamin as well as Judah). And she weeps for "Ephraim"—a symbol of the northern kingdom already in captivity.

But why would God begin a "Book of Consolation" with a repeated emphasis on the Babylonian conquest? Apparently, the Lord desired to assure the nation with double certainty that in spite of the impending horror—as excruciating as a difficult birthing— it would all give way to the actual birth of a new, united nation (Judah and Israel), a new beginning, a new age.

In the same manner, the end-time troubles that will face the last generation of God's people are only the birth pangs and "hard labor" that precedes the establishment of God's eternal kingdom of righteousness. Like Judah—and Christ—the end-time Christian must focus his faith on the "joy" that lies beyond the pain of birthing (see Hebrews 12:2).

"Jacob" will not only "be saved out" of this experience (Jeremiah 30:7), but "Rachel" will see her children return from their exile:

"Keep your voice from weeping, and your eyes from tears; for your work shall be rewarded, . . . and *they shall come back from the land of the enemy. . . . Your children shall come back to their own country*" (Jeremiah 31:16, 17, emphasis added). Rachel's descendants who would return from exile would include persons not only from the southern kingdom (Benjamin/Judah) but also from the northern kingdom as well (Ephraim/Israel). The Bible knows nothing about the so-called "ten lost tribes of Israel." Persian freedom opened the door for every descendant of Jacob and Rachel to return.

In the "Rachel" prophecy, the Lord singles out the exiled northern kingdom of Israel (under the name of Ephraim). He observes that their exile is accomplishing His design. "I have heard Ephraim bemoaning, 'Thou hast chastened me, and I was chastened, like an untrained calf; bring me back that I may be restored, for thou art the Lord my God' " (verse 18).

Then the Lord instructs Jeremiah to pen His reply to Ephraim/Israel's request. "Is Ephraim my dear son? Is he my darling child? For as often as I speak against him, I do remember him still. *Therefore my heart yearns for him; I will surely have mercy on him*, says the Lord" (verse 20, emphasis added). We do not know how many among the exiled northern tribes returned when the opportunity was given, but it is evident from the biblical data that some did indeed return (see Ezra 6:16, 17; Luke 2:36).

Marvelous grace

In spite of the debacle of Jacob and Rachel's descendants, God assures His wayward people of His unfailing grace. They didn't deserve it; sinners never deserve divine kindness. The Lord recalls the experience of their liberation from slavery: "Thus says the Lord: 'The people who survived the sword *found grace in the wilderness*; when Israel sought for rest' " (Jeremiah 31:2, emphasis added).

The armed might of Egypt, moving by horse and chariot, bore down on the escaping Israelites, fleeing on foot with wagons and slow-moving herds. But divine favor delivered them at the Red Sea, and they had "survived the sword."

Now, the Lord speaks again: "*I have loved you with an everlasting love;* therefore *I have continued my faithfulness to you. Again I will build you, and you shall be built, O virgin Israel*" (verses 3, 4, emphasis added). Grace had delivered the nation from Egyptian slavery; grace would deliver the nation once more—from Babylonian exile. Grace would transform her from a "harlot" to "virgin Israel"! A new beginning! Marvelous grace! How patient, how persevering—and how effective (see 2 Corinthians 5:17)!

Divine grace is never miserly. It is always lavish! If the cup of the wine of God's wrath fills up, even so, the cup of His mercy "overflows" (Jeremiah 25:15-18; Psalm 23:5). We can compile a summary of the bright promises from the "Book of Consolations" that would continue to glow through the long Babylonian night:

1. Submission to Babylon would not be permanent. God would break the Chaldean yoke and bonds (Jeremiah 30:8).

2. Remedial punishment, not national extinction, was God's objective (verse 11).

3. Like a shepherd, God would keep and bring them back safely to Zion—"the blind and the lame, the woman with child and her who is in travail, together; a great company, they shall return here" (see Jeremiah 31:8-10; see also chapters 32:37-39; 23:1-4).

4. The Lord would restore their spiritual "health" and would "heal" their wounded, sin-sick souls. Their enemies would no longer deridingly call the nation "an outcast" (Jeremiah 30:12-17). They would be forgiven (Jeremiah 33:6-8).

5. Jerusalem would be rebuilt (Jeremiah 30:18) and its commerce reactivated (Jeremiah 32:42-44). Flocks and herds would once more graze on the now-abandoned lands (Jeremiah 33:12, 13).

6. Songs of thanksgiving and the voices of merrymakers would be heard again (Jeremiah 30:19; 31:4), also the voices of the bridegroom and bride, and the singing of those who would bring their thank offerings to the temple (Jeremiah 33:10, 11). "They shall come and sing aloud on the height of Zion, and they shall be radiant over the goodness of the Lord. . . . My people shall be satisfied with my goodness" (Jeremiah 31:12-14).

7. God would replant the nation. "I will sow the house of Israel and the house of Judah with the seed of man. . . . I will watch over them to build and to plant" (Jeremiah 31:27, 28). "I will plant them in this land in faithfulness, *with all my heart and all my soul*" (Jeremiah 32:41, emphasis added). God expresses no reservation about His intentions from His side of the covenant relationship.

The Messianic age

The "Book of Consolation" should be called the "Book of Hope," for its pages are edged with the golden anticipation of the Messiah's advent! If ever a generation of God's people needed a few "stars" of hope to fix their faith upon, it was the one about to undergo the night of Babylonian captivity. The shadows of that dark experience were already gathering ominously about them when the Lord bade Jeremiah to announce that the Messianic age was at hand.

First would come the discipline of the captivity. Second, God would bring about their release and return to the homeland (see Jeremiah 30:8). Third, the Messiah would arrive, and the long-looked-for Messianic age would begin. God promised: "They [the returned, new Israel] shall serve the Lord their God and *David their king,* whom I will raise up for them" (Jeremiah 30:9, emphasis, added). How is this to be understood? Did God intend to raise David from the grave? Not at all. We are dealing with a Hebraic thought pattern that the Bible itself explains. God meant they would serve One who would come in "the spirit and power of David." Such a Person would be "the son of David"—the Messiah Himself! (Compare the similar concept of Elijah's return in Malachi 4:5 and Luke 1:17).

The Persians eventually restored the Jewish state, but they never restored the Davidic throne. In harmony with Ezekiel's forecast (Ezekiel 21:27), Jewish hopes centered on the Messiah, who, as David's son, would take the throne. The angel Gabriel endorsed that hope when he announced the birth of Jesus to the virgin Mary: "He will be great, and will be called the Son of the Most High; and the Lord God will give to him the throne of his father David, and he will reign over the house of Jacob for ever; and of his kingdom there will be no end" (Luke 1:32, 33).

In a second oracle pertaining to the restoration and the Messianic age, Jeremiah quoted God:

> Behold, the days are coming, says the Lord, when I will raise up for David a righteous Branch, and he shall reign as king and deal wisely, and shall execute justice and righteousness in the land. . . . And this is the name by which he will be called: "The Lord is our righteousness" (Jeremiah 23:5, 6).

Jeremiah's statement reads literally: "And this [is] His name [by] which He will be called: Yahweh, our righteousness." To call the Messiah by the divine title *Yahweh* is to imply His divinity (see Isaiah 9:6, 7). Thus, we seem to have in this passage a hint of the coming incarnation: the Messiah would have both human and divine aspects. His humanity would be reflected in His descent from David and His divinity in His covenant name *Yahweh*, the Eternal One (see Romans 1:3, 4).[3] God's righteousness becomes our righteousness through the Messiah (see Isaiah 45:22-25; Philippians 3:9).

Jeremiah's third major Messianic statement is recorded in chapter 33, verses 14 to 17. Verses 14 and 15 are similar to Jeremiah 23 verses 5 and 6 discussed above, except it is said that in that happy age to come, *Jerusalem* would be called "Yahweh, our righteousness" (verse 16, literal translation). This simply reflects God's ideal that in the coming era, the people would reflect the righteous character of the Messiah. According to Jeremiah, the believer who is in covenant relationship with God is "called by [His] name" (Jeremiah 14:9). In the Scriptures, God's "name" stands for His person and character attributes (see Exodus 34:5-7).

Then comes another thrilling promise: "David shall never lack a man to sit on the throne of the house of Israel, and the Levitical priests shall never lack a man in my presence to offer burnt offerings, to burn cereal offerings, and to make sacrifices for ever" (Jeremiah 33:17, 18).

We do not know in what manner God would have begun to fulfill this prophecy had Judah been true to its calling. But Jesus, as the Messiah, did assume permanently all the prerogatives of David and Levi (of kingship and priesthood) when, upon His ascension, He took His throne at the right hand of God as King-Priest in the heavenly sanctuary (see Hebrews 4:14-16; 5:5, 6; 8:1, 2) and began His Messianic reign (see 1 Corinthians 15:25; 1 Peter 3:22).

From the New Testament viewpoint, Jesus' Messianic reign from heaven fulfills the Messianic age (the Christian era) on earth. He rules in the worldwide kingdom of grace (see Hebrews 4:16; Luke 17:20, 21, margin). Christ's eternal kingdom of glory will not be realized until His return in majesty and power (see Matthew 6:9, 10; 25:31). Not until then will the great Messianic promises of a restored Davidic throne and kingdom meet their complete fulfillment.

But the major outlines of the Messianic picture were fulfilled in the actual appearance, ministry, death, resurrection, and ascension of Jesus of Nazareth as the Christ. At His enthronement in heaven as our King-Priest, there came the outpouring of the Holy Spirit as promised by the prophet Joel (see Joel 2:28-32; see also Peter's explanation, Acts 2:16-39; 5:31).

The appearing of the Messiah, the renewal of the covenant relationship on the basis of His solid accomplishments, and the outpouring of the Holy Spirit—all golden promises—assured despondent and dejected Judah that its finest hour still lay in its future, not its past! Every night has its dawning, and the rising of the Sun of Righteousness would bring a new day (see Malachi 4:2)!

The certainty of the promises

Two strongly worded promises in the "Book of Consolation" have led many Christians to believe that end-time Jewry will convert to the Christian faith. It is argued that this will result in a literal Jewish fulfillment of all the Old Testament promises.

The two promises are similar (see Jeremiah 31:35-37; 33:20-26). For lack of space, we select the major line of reasoning. God says, in sum, *if* the natural, celestial order (sun, moon, stars)—this fixed order—collapses, then the descendants of Israel will cease from being a nation before Me (see Jeremiah 31:35, 36).

Some people assert that since these cosmic arrangements are immutable, Israel is guaranteed an existence as a nation forever. Therefore, no sin or sins on Israel's part can in any manner nullify this kind of promise. No conditions are attached. It is admitted that Israel has "stumbled," but eventually Israel will "get its act together," so to speak, and all the promises made to national Israel in the Old Testament will find their fulfillment in them—not in the church.

While every sincere Christian would delight to see the conversion of every person of Jewish extraction or connection, this view simply misreads the biblical testimony on the subject. It fails to take into account several biblical facts:

1. These promises are made *from God's side only*. Nothing is said about the human response. Their purpose is to underscore *God's fidelity*.

2. God Himself has said in these same prophecies of Jeremiah that *His promises are conditional on the obedience of His people* (see Jeremiah 18:7-10).

3. The New Testament is clear that Jewish rejection of Jesus as the Messiah terminated their special relationship to God as His agents and that their privileges, responsibilities, and promises have become the heritage of the Christian church (composed of both Jewish and Gentile believers in Jesus as the Messiah). The new Israel (the church) now occupies the role that ancient Israel once did as God's agents. The door of salvation remains open to all peoples as long as human probation shall last. (See chapter 4 for texts and discussion.)

4. Simple political possession of "Holy Land" territory is not a fulfillment of Bible prophecy. The biblical conditions always require that the land be held in connection with a covenant relationship with God (see Psalm 105:6-11).

It is never a safe method of Bible study to isolate passages such as these promises from their general scriptural context. And we ignore at our peril the conditional nature of God's covenant promises. "*If* you will obey my voice and keep my covenant, you shall be my own possession among all peoples; for all the earth is mine" (Exodus 19:5, emphasis added).[4]

---

1. Eleanor L. Doan, comp., *The Speaker's Sourcebook* (Grand Rapids, Mich.: Zondervan Publishing House, 1960), 127.

2. Since Babylon's conquest of Judah is described as "the great day of the Lord" on Judah (Zephaniah 1:14-18; see also Joel 1:15), it is only natural for many Christians to see a parallel between Jeremiah 30:4-9 and the last great attack on the church. Just as ancient Babylon swept down to conquer the Jews (thus creating the time of Jacob's trouble/distress), so the prophecies indicate that the confederate forces of evil (end-time Babylon the Great—Revelation 17) will seek to destroy God's end-time people (see Revelation 12:17; 13:15-17), thereby creating another time of enormous stress for God's people. But the promise remains true in both instances: "He [Jacob] shall be saved out of it" (Jeremiah 30:7). (See Ellen G. White, *The Great Controversy* [Boise, Idaho: Pacific Press Publishing Association, 1950], 613-634).

3. Jesus argued for the deity and humanity of the Messiah from the Messianic Psalm 110 (see Matthew 22:41-46).

4. "The Jews had misinterpreted God's promise of eternal favor to Israel [Jeremiah 31:35-37 cited]. . . . They overlooked the conditions which God had specified. Before giving the promise, He had said, 'I will put My law in their inward parts, and write it in their hearts; and will be their God, and they shall be My people. . . . For I will forgive their iniquity, and I will remember their sin no more.' Jeremiah 31:33, 34. To a people in whose hearts His law is written, the favor of God is assured. They are one with Him. But the Jews had separated themselves from God. Because of their sins they were suffering under His judgments." (White, *The Desire of Ages*, 106). For helpful studies on the role of Israel and the interpretation of the Scriptures, see Hans K. LaRondelle, *The Israel of God in Prophecy* (Berrien Springs, Mich.: Andrews University Press, 1983; Gerhard F. Hasel, "Israel in Bible Prophecy," *Journal of the Adventist Theological Society*, 3 (Spring 1992): 120-155.

Chapter 12

The Collapse of a Nation

On January 15, 588 B.C., the Chaldean military forces drew a cordon of troops and siegeworks around Jerusalem (see Jeremiah 52:4). Thirty months later—July 19, 586 B.C.—when the defenders were weakened by battle losses, starved to the point of cannibalism, and ravaged by diseases—the battering rams finally breached the walls. Wildly yelling warriors swarmed into the streets of the capital everywhere, overwhelming pockets of resistance. Zedekiah's attempted flight from the beleaguered city failed, and the king and the remnants of his army were surrounded and captured near Jericho.

The collapse of the kingdom of Judah, of which Jerusalem was but a microcosm, was not due simply to the superior valor of Babylonian arms or the weakness of their opponents. The fact that Jerusalem endured a siege of two and a half years testifies to the tenacity of its defenders. The nation's downfall was sure to come. Like other ruined political states, Judah's physical collapse was due to its moral deterioration. The nation was rotten at its core, from top to bottom, from prince to peasant.

It is remarkable that the only person (other than Jeremiah himself) who acknowledged the real reason for Judah's fate was not a believing Jew, but a pagan soldier, Nebuzaradan, the captain of the guard. When he released Jeremiah from his bonds (see Jeremiah 40:1), he observed: "The Lord your God pronounced this evil against this place; the Lord has brought it about, and has done as he said. Because you sinned against the Lord, and did not obey his voice, this thing has come upon you" (verses 2 and 3). Like another pagan soldier, who alone acknowledged Christ's deity on the day He died (see Mark 15:39), Nebuzaradan made a correct assessment of Judah's problem: The nation had "sinned against the Lord."

King Zedekiah

King Zedekiah was one of the most ill-prepared persons in both training and force of character to occupy the throne of David.

The Lord's patience with the bewildered young man is amazing. While the siege ground on, Jeremiah arrived at the palace with a special message. He informed Zedekiah that Nebuchadnezzar would capture and burn the city and that Zedekiah himself would be captured, interviewed by Nebuchadnezzar, and taken to Babylon. But he promised: "You shall not die by the sword. You shall die in peace. And as spices were burned for your fathers, the former kings who were before you, so men shall burn spices for you and lament for you, saying, 'Alas, lord!' For I have spoken the word, says the Lord" (34:4, 5). But this assurance failed to stabilize the vacillating monarch.

In response to an earlier query from Zedekiah, Jeremiah had advised surrender (see Jeremiah 21:1-10). Now again, the king sends the request: "Pray for us to the Lord our God" (Jeremiah 37:3). About this time the Chaldeans lifted the siege. They had received intelligence that the Egyptian Pharaoh Hophra was advancing from the south for the relief of embattled Judah. As the Babylonian soldiery broke camp and withdrew to meet the new enemy, it seemed that the Lord had truly "answered" the prayers of the besieged!

But the Lord directed Jeremiah to reply with a chilling retort: Pharaoh's army would retreat—in other words, would never shoot an arrow in their behalf—and the Chaldeans would return and take Jerusalem. Don't deceive yourselves by thinking that "the Chaldeans will surely stay away from us." And then Jeremiah added, in hyperbolic terms: "Even if you should defeat the whole army of Chaldeans . . . and there remained of them only wounded men, every man in his tent, they would rise up and burn this city with fire" (verses 9, 10).

Because the siege had lifted, Jeremiah decided to return home to Anathoth on some business matter. He was recognized in the gate of Benjamin and accused of deserting to the enemy. Despite his protests to the contrary, the authorities arrested him. He was beaten and imprisoned (verses 11-15), apparently with the approval of

Zedekiah (Jeremiah 32:1-5), who was miffed at the prophet for predicting his capture (see Jeremiah 34:1-5).

Jeremiah suffered a good deal in the harsh dungeon where the princes had incarcerated him. He had been there "many days," when unexpectedly Zedekiah had him brought to the palace for an interview. Once more the cowardly king asked, "Is there any word from the Lord?" (Jeremiah 37:17). Yes, was the prophet's forthright answer. "You shall be delivered into the hand of the king of Babylon." Then Jeremiah demanded that the king tell what wrong he had done to him or the court that he should be so ill-treated. He requested not to be confined to the dungeon again, so Zedekiah had him placed in the court of the guard (verses 20, 21).

A short time later, when the princes clamored for Jeremiah's death because he encouraged the people to surrender to the Chaldeans, Zedekiah gave in. But the prophet was rescued from the death pit by the Ethiopian Ebedmelech (see Jeremiah 38:1-13). The rescue led to Zedekiah's last interview with Jeremiah—a secret one, for which the prophet was brought to the "third entrance of the temple" (see verses 14-28).

Once more the king desired to know God's intentions. But this time the prophet demurred: "If I tell you, you will put me to death, and if I give you counsel, you won't listen." In response, the fickle king "swore" in the name of Yahweh that he would not allow his execution, but he refused the counsel to surrender (verses 15-22).

Zedekiah's interest in receiving a "word from the Lord" was only a sham. He stubbornly refused to follow God's counsel to save either his own life or that of his household and city. A little later the city fell, and he was captured. He stood in chains before Nebuchadnezzar at the latter's field headquarters in Syria and watched in horror as the Chaldean guards butchered his sons. Then his own eyes were gouged out, and he was bound in fetters for removal to Babylon (see Jeremiah 39:5-7). His wives and concubines and children were turned over to the brutal soldiery (see Jeremiah 38:21-23). A month later the temple, palaces, and houses of Jerusalem were burned to the ground, and the great walls of the city were thrown down (see Jeremiah 52:12-14).

These terrible events so shattered the Jewish mind that afterward, on their anniversaries, the Jews fasted and mourned on the tenth month (siege's beginning); fourth month (fall of the city);

fifth month (burning of the city and temple); and seventh month (murder of Gadaliah, the governor; remnants' flight to Egypt).

The man-made fasts were kept for nearly seventy years—from 586 B.C. to 518/517 B.C. (see Zechariah 7:3, 5; 8:19; 2 Kings 25:1-9; Jeremiah 52:12-16; 41:1, 2). If such "faithfulness" in mourning and repenting and confession of sin had taken place during Judah's previous forty years, the discipline of the captivity would never have been needed. God's desire would have been fulfilled.

The third commandment

Crises reveal character. In the Judeo-Babylonian conflict, Zedekiah's weaknesses all came to the fore. In the prophecies of Ezekiel, the Lord zeroes in on one sin for which He held the king highly accountable: perjury. Many moderns take this universal sin lightly, but God does not.

Perjury—swearing under oath to what is untrue or violating a solemn promise made under oath—is (for a believer in God) a direct violation of the third commandment: "You shall not take the name of the Lord your God in vain; for the Lord will not hold him guiltless who takes his name in vain" (Exodus 20:7). God exempts the judicial oath (see Deuteronomy 6:13; see also the example of Jesus—Matthew 26:63, 64) but forbids a false oath in His name (see Leviticus 19:11) and the unnecessary oaths of ordinary conversation (see Matthew 5:33-37).

By the year 597 B.C., when Zedekiah took the throne, Nebuchadnezzar had come to know something about the character and power of the true God. Daniel's remarkable revelation and interpretation of his dream and his association with Shadrach, Meshach, and Abednego in the governance of Babylon had taught him much about Israel's God. For about five years, he observed their loyalty both to their Deity and to the empire (see Daniel 2:46-49).

This led Nebuchadnezzar to take a different approach with Zedekiah than he had with Jehoiakim, whom he had put under tribute (see 2 Kings 24:1). This time the Chaldean placed Zedekiah under oath, to "swear by God"—Israel's God—Yahweh, the Creator of heaven and earth (see 2 Chronicles 36:13). Zedekiah evidently took a similar oath when he reaffirmed his allegiance to the Babylonian crown in his fourth year (see Jeremiah 51:59).[1]

Zedekiah's loyalty covenant, which he so easily confirmed in the name of God, the Lord took most seriously. In God's discussion of it with Ezekiel (see Ezekiel 17:11-21), He mentions the covenant Zedekiah had made with Nebuchadnezzar six times, and exclaims: "Can he break the covenant and yet escape?" (verse 15). Zedekiah broke his covenant by forming an alliance with Egypt and by declaring Judah's independence from Babylon.

But what is remarkable about Zedekiah's covenant oath is that since he affirmed his promise in the Lord's name, God viewed the oath as though He Himself had made it. By breaking covenant with Nebuchadnezzar—sworn to in God's name—Zedekiah had not only perjured himself but *had also defamed the name and character of the true God!* "As I live, surely *my oath* which he despised, and *my covenant* which he broke, I will requite upon his head," the Lord declared, "and I will bring him to Babylon . . . for *the treason he has committed against me*" (Ezekiel 17:19, 20, emphasis added).

This important covenant was not the only one that Zedekiah broke in these crisis years. When Jerusalem lay under its final siege, he evidently thought to secure God's favor (or did he fear Jewish betrayers?) by making a solemn covenant to release all Hebrew slaves and give them their liberty (see Jeremiah 34:8-10). The Mosaic law requiring the release of Hebrew slaves at the end of six years of service had been disregarded for years (verse 14; see also Exodus 21:2).

But when the Chaldeans temporarily lifted the siege to meet the Egyptian relief expedition, the king, his princes, and others broke their promises—sworn to in the name of the Lord—and enslaved their former servants. Once more, God declared that such fickle behavior "profaned my name" (verse 16) and declared that the men who had "transgressed *my covenant*" would be delivered over into the hands of their enemies, and many of them would be slain (verses 18-22, emphasis added).

The lesson of Zedekiah and the third commandment is writ large for Christians who "take the name of the Lord" when they are baptized in the name of the Trinity (see Matthew 28:19), a covenant promise and act in itself. Baptism calls for reverent living before God. Christian baptism and the third commandment impact not only on all agreements, contracts, wedding vows, and all other solemn promises but also upon every act of the Christian life. Every day we face the question: Do we bring honor or dishonor to the God whose name we bear? It is a high privilege to be a follower of the true, living God, but it is a vocation we must take seriously, "for

the Lord will not hold him guiltless who takes his name in vain"
(Exodus 20:7).

Flight to Egypt

Permitted by Nebuzaradan to go with him to Babylon or to live
wherever he chose, Jeremiah decided to settle in Mizpah, a town
about eight miles north of Jerusalem, the new seat of government
for the Jews left in the land. Gedaliah, the son of Prince Ahikam,
who years before had rescued Jeremiah from certain death, had
now been appointed the governor of the land (see Jeremiah 40:4-6;
26:24). Jeremiah would stay and support him.

The governor's first task was to pacify the scattered field forces—
small groupings of officers and troops—that the Babylonians did
not attempt to ferret out of the mountains and caves and deserts of
Judah. These officers and their men now came to Mizpah. Gedaliah
welcomed them kindly and promised full amnesty. He urged them,
as the season was advancing, to "gather wine and summer fruits
and oil, and store them in your vessels, and dwell in your cities
that you have taken." He would represent them to the Babylonian
government (Jeremiah 40:9, 10).

As news of permanent peace in Judah spread to the neighboring
countries, refugees in Moab, Ammon, Edom, and other lands began
to return to their former homes (verse 12). Although the national
state no longer existed, peace had returned to the land and its more
humble residents. So it seemed.

The governor was warned in secret by Johanan, one of the field
officers, that Ishmael, "of the royal family," was being urged by
Baalis, the king of the Ammonites, to assassinate the governor. The
informer requested permission to kill Ishmael, but Gedaliah refused. He could not credit such a thing and charged Johanan with
falsehood (verses 13-16). But two months after the Babylonian
withdrawal, Gedaliah, his staff, the Chaldean garrison, and seventy men who had come to town on their way to pray at the ruined
temple site were murdered by the assassin's sword (see Jeremiah
41:1-10).

Ishmael gathered the Jews in the Mizpah area, including
Jeremiah, and forced them to accompany him to the kingdom of
Ammon, across the Jordan. But Johanan and other field men soon
heard of the foul deed and intercepted the murderer. In the ensuing
skirmish, Ishmael and eight of his men escaped and continued

their flight to Ammon. Johanan and the other officers and troops gathered the rescued Jews and established temporary living arrangements in a village near Bethlehem. Fearing that the overthrow of Gedaliah and the garrison would bring harsh reprisals from the Babylonians, they determined to flee to Egypt.

"Pray to the Lord your God for us," the officers and the people asked Jeremiah, "that the Lord . . . may show us the way we should go, and the thing that we should do" (Jeremiah 42:2, 3). Although they piously agreed to do whatever the Lord directed (verses 5, 6), they were secretly fully fixed in their purpose to go down to Egypt. The people really did not want God's guidance, only His approval of their plans. Jeremiah agreed to intercede for them and to withhold nothing that the Lord revealed (verse 4), but he must have wondered about their unusual interest and desire to obey the word of the Lord.

Ten days passed before the Lord communicated His will. Perhaps the lapse of time was permitted to let the initial panic over reprisals dissipate. Then God sent an encouraging message: "If you will remain in this land, then I will build you up and not pull you down; I will plant you, and not pluck you up" (verse 10). Furthermore, God assured them not to fear reprisals; He would cause Babylon to leave them in the land (verses 11, 12).

But, of course, the Lord had read the real intent of their "prayer." If they thought to escape war and famine by flight to Egypt (contrary to God's will for this remnant), the Babylonian sword would overtake them there. "All the men who set their faces to go to Egypt to live there shall die by the sword, by famine, and by pestilence. . . . You shall see this place no more" (verses 17, 18).

Exposed by God's revelation, their facade fell away. A bitter spirit surfaced as the officers angrily charged Jeremiah: "You are telling a lie. The Lord our God did not send you to say, 'Do not go to Egypt to live there'; but Baruch [Jeremiah's secretary] . . . has set you against us, to deliver us into the hand of the Chaldeans, that they may kill us or take us into exile in Babylon" (Jeremiah 43:2, 3).

Jeremiah made no reply; he had faithfully transmitted God's message. Johanan and his officers gave the orders to pack for their trek to Egypt, and a few days later the band of refugees, including Jeremiah and Baruch, set off for Egypt, arriving in due time at the fortress city of Tahpanhes in the eastern Delta (verses 4-7).

While the refugees rested (possibly waiting for permission to settle in the land), the Lord directed Jeremiah to enact another parabolic message. Having laid a number of paving stones near the entrance to Pharaoh's palace, he predicted to the watching Jews that Nebuchadnezzar would eventually march on Egypt and, placing "his throne above these stones," would direct his invasion forces. "He shall come and smite the land of Egypt," killing, pillaging, and burning. The war that the refugees sought to escape, in their stubborn disobedience to God's will, would overtake them in the land of their supposed refuge (verses 8-13).

The people's choice

The events described and predicted in chapter 44 occurred between Nebuchadnezzar's nineteenth year (the fall of Jerusalem/Judah, 586 B.C.—2 Kings 25:8, 9) and his thirty-seventh year (an invasion of Egypt—568 B.C.—Jeremiah 43:8-13; 46:13-26; Ezekiel 29:17-20), a span of eighteen years.[2]

This encounter between Jeremiah and the refugees must have occurred a few years after their entry into Egypt, since the Jews were by then living not only in Migdol and Tahpanhes (in the northeastern Delta region) but also at Memphis (at the apex of the Delta, near modern Cairo) and in Pathros (the extreme southern part of the nation, also known as Upper Egypt). This particular confrontation appears to have taken place at some location in Pathros (see Jeremiah 44:15).

Jeremiah found it incredible that having experienced God's judgments on their idolatry in Judah, the refugees would now turn to the worship of the Egyptian gods (verses 2-10). In the face of such perversity, he declared God's determined judgment on them:

> I will punish those who dwell in the land of Egypt, as I have punished Jerusalem, with the sword, with famine, and with pestilence, so that none of the remnant of Judah who have come to live in the land of Egypt shall escape or survive or return to the land of Judah, . . . except some fugitives (verses 13, 14).

Their response pierced the heart of the prophet who had spent an entire lifetime endeavoring to save his nation from ruin. " 'We will not listen to you,' " the people replied. We will worship the gods as we have vowed to do, especially the queen of heaven. We had plenty and prosperity when we worshiped her in Judah, but we have had nothing but trouble since Josiah's reform (verses 15-19).

In the brazen and resistant attitudes of these refugees, we see an Old Testament example of the "unpardonable sin" (see Matthew 12:22-37). Here, the covenant people denounced the worship of the true and living God as false and troubling, but the worship of false gods as true and conducive to prosperity! White had become black, and black had become white!

But Jeremiah would not leave them with their twisted interpretation of Judah's past history. For the last time, he carefully explained that the national ruin had come about because of their sins against the true God—their covenant God. The Lord could no longer bear with their insolent and defying ways, and He had disciplined them by permitting the Babylonian conquest (verses 20-23).

Go on, he said, and worship your gods, but know that you have come once more under divine judgment, and you will be consumed by a war you thought to avoid. "I will punish you in this place," the Lord said. As a sign of the certainty of their fate, God said He would give Pharaoh Hophra—Judah's ally and their protector—into the hands of his enemies, even as He had given Zedekiah over to Nebuchadnezzar (verses 29-30).

Some time later a military coup forced Hophra to accept his army commander Ahmose (Amasis) as a co-regent on his throne. A bloody battle between the supporters of the two rulers resulted in Hophra's death. When Nebuchadnezzar arrived at the frontiers of Egypt with his armies, he faced the forces of Amasis. At this point a veil of silence falls over the history of the times, but we can be sure that "the word of the Lord" regarding the Jewish refugees and Nebuchadnezzar's invasion of Egypt took place as Jeremiah predicted (see Jeremiah 43:8-13). The Lord's word never fails (see Isaiah 40:8).

---

1. "Had Zedekiah respected . . . his covenant oath, his loyalty would have had a profound influence on the minds of many who were watching the conduct of those who claimed to reverence the name and to cherish the honor of the God of the Hebrews. But Judah's king lost sight of his high privilege of bringing honor to the name of the living God." (White, *Prophets and Kings*, [Boise, Idaho: Pacific Press Publishing Association, 1943]) 447.

2. A fragmentary historical text records a Babylonian invasion of Egypt in Nebuchadnezzar's thirty-seventh year. This is generally thought to be the fulfillment of Jeremiah's prediction. The text reads in part: "In the 37th year, Nebuchadnezzar, king of Babylon marched against Egypt to deliver a battle" (see *ANET*, 2nd ed., 308).

Chapter 13

The Ministry of Sorrow

The ministry of sorrow is not an experience we crave, yet it often succeeds in righting the imbalance of our lives. A great sorrow usually stops us in our tracks and forces us to think about the brevity and fragility of life, about our priorities, about what is really important to our happiness.

Sometimes our deepest griefs find best expression in poetic form—such as in elegies or laments. The most extensive grouping of elegies in Scripture is the book of Lamentations itself. However, these moving poems express poignant sorrow not over the death of a human being but over the demise of Jerusalem and the nation of Judah in 586 B.C. *National* suffering rather than personal suffering are in the forefront of these laments, although couched at times in personal terms.[1]

In the Hebrew Bible (the Christian's Old Testament), the book of Lamentations is simply titled by its first word, *How* (*'êkāh*). No author is listed. However, in the Greek Septuagint (LXX), the Greek translation of the Hebrew Bible made by Jews in the third to second centuries, B.C., the collection of five poems opens with this statement: "And it came to pass after Israel had been taken into captivity and Jerusalem laid waste, that Jeremiah sat weeping and uttered this lament over Jerusalem and said . . ."

In our common Bibles, each chapter of the book of Lamentations contains a complete poem. Excepting chapter 3, each poem is just twenty-two verses long; chapter 3 is a multiple of twenty-two. Jeremiah devised the lamentations in the literary form of an acrostic, employing the twenty-two characters of the Hebrew alphabet. Poems 1 to 4 are true acrostics. The initial letter of the first word of each stanza begins with a letter of the alphabet in its natural sequence. And so the elegies are arranged something like our childhood alphabet books: A is for apple, B is for ball, etc.

Lamentation 1

The lament begins on a somber note to describe the ruined condition of Jerusalem (verses 1-11). Jeremiah compares the city to a grieving widow. "How lonely sits the city that was full of people! How like a widow has she become. . . . She weeps bitterly in the night, tears on her cheeks" (verses 1, 2). Later in the poem, the "widow" is personified and soliloquizes upon her desperate condition (verses 12-22).

Inspiration does not select the figure of "widowhood" to imply her "husband's" decease, for God—Judah's true husband (see Isaiah 54:5)—is not dead! Rather, the symbol is chosen to emphasize Jerusalem's desolate condition, her abandonment by former "friends," her aloneness (verse 2), loss of position (verses 1, 6), and removal to a foreign land (verses 3, 4, 5).

Jeremiah recalls the loss of the temple and the cessation of the yearly festivals (verses 4, 10). In spite of Judah's gross idolatry, the temple was the pride of the nation. Through Ezekiel, God had predicted its destruction in terms of its beauty and the national pride: "Behold, I will profane my sanctuary, the pride of your power, the delight of your eyes, and the desire of your soul" (Ezekiel 24:21). Now, widowed Jerusalem contemplates in amazed sorrow that "she has seen the nations invade her sanctuary"—the pagan peoples who once were forbidden to enter its holy precincts (verse 10)!

Again, Jeremiah recalls the gloating of the victors over the collapse of the city. "When her people fell into the hand of the foe, and there was none to help her, the foe gloated over her, mocking at her downfall" (verse 7). It takes a courageous person, like a Daniel, to remain true to God in all circumstances, but how embarrassing to endure mocking when it is your own sin that has brought it on! Now, as forewarned in the covenant curses (see Deuteronomy 28:44), the national enemies had become "the head," and Judah, "the tail."

But the weeping prophet is faithful to his task. There is a reason for Judah's widowlike desolation: "The Lord has made her suffer for the multitude of her transgressions" (verse 5). "Jerusalem sinned grievously. . . . She took no thought of her doom" (verses 8, 9).

Heedlessly, the nation played the harlot, broke covenant with God and spurned His grace, and came under divine judgment "as women who break wedlock and shed blood" (Ezekiel 16:38).

In the second half of the lament, Jeremiah places the speech—the sobbing admissions and confessions—on the lips of widowed Jerusalem. Perhaps he was inspired by the Spirit to teach God's people in this manner how to pray true prayers of contrition and repentance.

The "widow" asks supposed passersby: "Is it nothing to you, all you who pass by? Look and see if there is any sorrow like my sorrow which was brought upon me, which the Lord inflicted on the day of his fierce anger" (verse 12). Jerusalem "speaks" like Naomi, who lost three loved ones through natural causes but who attributed her plight to God (see Ruth 1:20, 21).

But in verses 18 to 20 the "widow" of Judah makes a frank and free confession: *"The Lord is in the right, for I have rebelled against his word. . . .* Behold, O Lord, for I am in distress, my soul is in tumult, my heart is wrung within me, *because I have been very rebellious.* In the street the sword bereaves; in the house it is like death" (emphasis added).

Thus, throughout the first Lamentation, the nation sobs out her dismay and hurt, and intermingled with her tears come the fragmentary confessions of a broken heart. There is no appeal now to the false "queen of heaven" (see Jeremiah 2:27, 28). In her distress, widowed Jerusalem instinctively calls upon the Lord, her only Saviour (verses 9, 11).

Lamentation 2

If a widow's desolations composed the major theme of the first lament, then destruction is the emphasis of the second. True to his Hebraic heritage, Jeremiah describes the devastation of the nation, temple, and people as "an act of God"! Verses 1 to 9 describe the Lord as a mighty, relentless warrior who has toppled the proud "daughter of Zion" and laid her palaces and strongholds in ruin.

This passage is a good illustration of the Hebrew thought pattern that attributes all actions to God. Consequently, God is often said to do things that the Western mind would say He permitted to be done, or did not prevent. In this case, God withdrew His blessing and protection from His covenant-breaking people, thereby allowing the Babylonians to sweep in. But in the lament, the offended and sinned-against Lord is depicted as drawing "his bow like an enemy" to slay the impenitent armies of His people (verse 4). In broad strokes Jeremiah sketches the impact of divine wrath on the sin-hardened nation:

1. The Lord humbled proud Judah. "The Lord in his anger . . . has cast down from heaven to earth the splendor of Israel. . . . He has brought down to the ground in dishonor the kingdom and its rulers" (verses 1, 2).

Judah's national wisdom, greatness, and prosperity lay in whole-hearted obedience to God's will (see Deuteronomy 4:5-8). It had no inherent greatness and deceived itself into thinking it could chart its own course, independent of God (see Jeremiah 10:23).

2. The Lord decimated Judah's armies, "all the might of Israel" (verses 3, 5).

3. The Lord reduced the strongholds and palaces to rubble (verses 2, 5).

4. The Lord laid His temple in ruins, "his footstool" (verses 1, 6, 7). God's "footstool" is probably to be understood as a reference to the temple and not simply to the ark of the covenant (see 1 Chronicles 28:2; Psalm 99:5). The figure preserves picturesquely the vertical dimension between the earthly and heavenly temples. God is figuratively described as sitting on His throne in the heavenly sanctuary with His feet resting upon the earthly sanctuary as upon a footstool.

But Judah had so corrupted God's system of worship, He did not hesitate to smash the great edifice reared to His honor as if it were but a flimsy shed (verse 6). "The Lord has scorned his altar, disowned his sanctuary; he has delivered it into the hand of the enemy" (verse 7; see also Psalm 74:4-8; 79:1-13).

A mere building—even a dedicated building—does not hallow human worship. It is the attitude of the heart that counts with God—as Jesus later said: "God is spirit, and those who worship him must worship in spirit and truth" (John 4:24). When a congregation loses the true spirit of obedience and worship, God's presence departs the premises of their "temple," no matter how beautiful its appointments or how correct the congregation's theory of belief.

5. The Lord razed Jerusalem and broke down its walls and gates (verses 8, 9).

6. The Lord cut—so it seemed—**the cord of communication with His people** (verse 9). No national administration advised the people; both were in exile. No priesthood functioned to unfold God's messages from "the law"—His Word (see Malachi 2:7). And the false prophets—as it was now evident (see Lamentations 2:14)—had no vision from the Lord (verse 9). Only silence now. Jeremiah's own task in Judah had essentially ceased. The new deportees would eventually hear in captivity—for a little while—the voice of Ezekiel and, perhaps, of Daniel.

At this point, Jeremiah seems to break down at the horror of it. "My eyes are spent with weeping; my soul is in tumult" (verse 11). He wonders what he can say by way of comfort to the wretched people (verse 13). But he is impelled by the Spirit to remind them that the divine hand was involved all along in this terrible discipline. "The Lord has done what he purposed, has carried out his threat; as he ordained long ago, he has demolished without pity; he has made the enemy rejoice over you, and exalted the might of your foes" (verse 17).

This second lamentation may have been written during the actual events of siege, or possibly between the fall of the capital and its burning a month later. If so, it is easy to see why the prophet makes an abrupt change at verse 18, calling on the distressed Jews to cry out at once to the Lord: "Cry aloud to the Lord! O daughter of Zion! Let tears stream down like a torrent day and night! . . . Arise, cry out in the night. . . . Pour out your heart like water before the presence of the Lord!" (verses 18, 19).

What would be subject of their sobbing supplications? "Lift your hands to him," implores the prophet, in behalf of the children who are collapsing in the streets for lack of food (verse 19). Show Him the bodies of young and old, maidens and youth, lying in the dust of the streets, slain by the sword (verse 21).

The eyewitness can only confess that the carnage seems like a giant sacrifice. "Thou didst invite as to the day of an appointed feast . . . and on the day of the anger of the Lord none escaped or survived" (verse 22). This kind of language recalls the prediction of Zephaniah, one of Jeremiah's contemporaries: "Be silent before the Lord God! For the day of the Lord is at hand; the Lord has prepared a sacrifice and consecrated his guests. And on the day of the Lord's sacrifice—'I will punish'" (Zephaniah 1:7, 8). The slain Jews were the sacrifice; the Babylonians, the guests. But from the midst of this holocaust the weeping pleas of the survivors seem to be asking God, Has not sufficient expiation been made?

Lamentation 3

Commentators differ on the identity of "the man" in verse 1. We assume that he is Jeremiah, who, in his speech and sufferings, personifies the sufferings of the nation at that time. "I am the man who has seen affliction under the rod of [God's] wrath" (verse 1). In the first twenty verses the prophet describes—largely in a figurative manner—the national afflictions as though he personally had received these blows from God's "rod": "Driven" into the dark (verse 2); skin and flesh wasted, bones broken (verse 4); enveloped in bitterness and tribulation (verse 5); path of escape blocked (verse 9); pounced upon and torn in pieces by wild animals (verses 10, 11); shot and pierced with arrows (verses 12, 13); filled with bitterness; the laughingstock of the nations (verses 14, 15); teeth broken on gravel; cowering in the ashes (verse 16).

As a result of his severe afflictions, he "is bereft of peace" and has "forgotten what happiness is." "Gone is my glory, and my expectation from the Lord" (verses 17, 18), Jeremiah moans in his role-play of the nation.

With verse 21 the tone dramatically changes. Suddenly the poem breaks away from the morose clouds of lament and languishing and leaps into the glorious sunshine of hope! The suffering prophet begins to recall three important aspects of God's character that he had forgotten in his misery (verse 21).

1. God is faithful, unchanging, dependable (verses 22, 23). In Jesus' parable of the lost boy (see Luke 15), it is this central truth of the father's faithful, unchanging nature that brought the sinning prodigal home again. Although he has fallen low and has disgraced the family name, he is sure his father still loves him. This great truth Jeremiah now seeks to impress upon his bewildered countrymen: *"The steadfast love of the Lord never ceases,* his mercies never come to an end; they are new every morning; *great is thy faithfulness"* (emphasis added).

2. God will respond to those who "wait for him" (verses 24-30). Since humanity is of God's creating, it is an indisputable fact that we are dependent upon Him. He is our "portion"—the sole source of our lives (see Acts 17:28). The penitent can with confidence cast himself upon the mercies of God and "hope in him" (verse 24).

The promise of response is certain. "The Lord is good to those who *wait* for him, *to the soul that seeks him.* It is good that one *should wait quietly* for the salvation of the Lord" (verses 25, 26, emphasis added). To "wait" for the Lord does not mean to sit idly in a chair by the fireplace, waiting for the Lord to ring the doorbell! To "wait on the Lord" is to "seek him" (verse 25) actively with contrition, humility, repentance and confession of sin (verses 28, 29)—accepting the consequences of our past sinning, even as we turn away from its practice (verse 30).

3. God disciplines His people with compassion (verses 31-39). Once more the prophet recalls the twin nature of Israel's God: He is both just and merciful. There is purpose in His discipline—always for our good! "The Lord will not cast off for ever, but, though he cause grief, he will have compassion according to the abundance of his steadfast love; for he does not willingly afflict or grieve the sons of men" (verses 31-33). In the light of God's gracious purposes, Jeremiah asks: "Why should a living man complain . . . about the punishment of his sins?" (verse 39).

As the Revised Standard Version translates the elegy, the remainder of the verses (verses 40-66) composes for the most part a prayer by Jeremiah (representing the nation). The prayer recalls past sins, their consequences, and an appeal to God, concluding with a request that the national enemies be requited also for their cruelty and taunts.

Lamentation 4

A large portion of this lamentation bewails the horrible effects of the siege-induced famine (verses 3-10). Infants at the breast died when their mother's milk dried up; children begged in vain for food (verse 4). Those accustomed to feasting "on dainties" perished in the streets (verse 5). Previously well-fed princes are no longer recognized in the streets, with "their skin . . . shriveled upon their bones . . . as dry as wood" (verse 8). "Compassionate women . . . boiled their own children" for "their food" (verse 10).

The prophet believed that the punishment of Judah was worse than that of Sodom. Sodom "was overthrown in a moment," but Jewish suffering went on for months, both during and after the siege (verse 6). "Happier were the victims of the sword," he said, "than the victims of hunger, who pined away, stricken by want of the fruits of the field" (verse 9).

In Lamentations 2, verse 14, Jeremiah had referred to the deceptive visions and misleading oracles of the false prophets. Now, in the fourth lamentation, they are fully exposed, along with a wicked priesthood, as the primary cause for the downfall of the nation. "*This* was for the sins of her prophets and the iniquities of her priests, who shed in the midst of her the blood of the righteous" (verse 13, emphasis added).

If every priest and so-called prophet had united to seek the Lord, to teach the people the will of God from the Scriptures, and to call the nation to repentance, Josiah's revival and reformation would have succeeded. But they not only confirmed the people in their sins (see Ezekiel 13:22) and falsely prophesied of peace (see Jeremiah 14:13), but also joined the people in their sinful practices (see Jeremiah 6:13; Ezekiel 8:11-13, 16).

In the ruin of the city and nation, the survivors now see these religious leaders as deceivers for the first time—and guilty of the blood of the people slain in this terrifying war—the people whom they had deliberately misled (verse 13). The outraged survivors turn on them, driving them away as lepers. "Away! Unclean! . . . So they became fugitives and wanderers; men said among the nations, 'They shall stay with us no longer.' The Lord himself has scattered them" (verses 15, 16).

Sooner or later the false prophet, teacher, or leader is exposed. And the duped become their most bitter enemies. But it is usually too late, and both the deceiver and the deceived perish together.

Lamentation 5

The last lamentation is a prayer—a prayer reciting again the various indignities the nation is suffering under Chaldean domination. The prophet pleads with God to "remember . . . what has befallen us; behold, and see our disgrace!" (verse 1). In biblical parlance, "to remember" something means not merely to recall the matter to the consciousness, but *to act*. In this instance, the petitioner desires God to ameliorate the situation (see Exodus 6:5, 6).

The supplicant acknowledges without rationalizations the cause for the national suffering and reproach: "The crown has fallen from our head; woe to us, for we have sinned!" (verse 16). But he also recognizes God's eternity: "Thou, O Lord, dost reign for ever; thy throne endures to all generations" (verse 19). The implication is that though *this* generation of Judah, being mortal, will die—many on foreign soil—yet God will outlive both them and their enemies. And the plea is that God, at His appointed time, will remember in mercy the nation and will act in its behalf in a favorable manner.

"Restore us to thyself, O Lord," Jeremiah pleads, "that we may be restored!" (verse 21). And, faithful as ever to His promises, God did! (see Jeremiah 29:13, 14).

---

1. The Targum on Lamentations attributes the poems to "Jeremiah the prophet and chief priest." (The Targums are ancient, interpretive Aramaic translations of most of the books of the Hebrew Bible.) The Babylonian Talmud *Baba Bathra* 15a likewise assigns authorship to Jeremiah as well as various rabbinic passages that cite the Lamentations with the formula, "Jeremiah said." See *ISBE*, 3:65, for LXX translation cited above and discussion of authorship.

Suggested Reading

Bromiley, Geoffrey, Everett F. Harrison, Ronald K. Harrison, William Sanford Lasora, eds. *International Standard Bible Encyclopedia, The*. Revised Edition. 4 vols. Grand Rapids, Mich.: William B. Eerdmans Publishing Company, 1979-1988.

Brueggemann, Walter. *To Pluck Up, to Tear Down—A Commentary on the Book of Jeremiah 1-25*. *International Theological Commentary*, edited by Fredrich C. Holmgren, et al. Grand Rapids, Mich.: William B. Eerdmans Publishing Company, 1988.

Day, David. *Jeremiah*. Leicester, England: InterVarsity Press, 1987.

Feinberg, Charles L. *Jeremiah*. Vol. 6 of *The Expositor's Bible Commentary*, edited by Frank E. Gaebelein. Grand Rapids, Mich.: Zondervan Publishing House, 1986.

Harrison, R. K. *Jeremiah and Lamentations. Tyndale Old Testament Commentaries*, edited by D. J. Wiseman, Leicester, England: InterVarsity Press, 1973.

Horn, Siegfried H., et al. *Seventh-day Adventist Bible Dictionary* Revised Edition, edited by Raymond H. Woolsey. Washington, D.C.: Review and Herald Publishing Association, 1979.

Kidner, Derek. *The Message of Jeremiah. The Bible Speaks Today* series, edited by J. A. Motyer. Leicester, England: InterVarsity Press, 1987.

Morgan, G. Campbell. *Studies in the Prophecy of Jeremiah*. Reprint Edition. Old Tappan, N.J.: Fleming H. Revell Company, 1969.

Nichol, Francis D., Raymond F. Cottrell, Don F. Neufeld, eds. *Isaiah to Malachi. Seventh-day Adventist Bible Commentary*. Vol. 4. Washington, D.C.: Review and Herald Publishing Association, 1977.

Peterson, Eugene H. *Run With the Horses*. Downers Grove, Ill.: InterVarsity Press, 1983.

Spence, H. D. M., and Joseph S. Exell, eds. *Pulpit Commentary, The*. Vols. 25, 26, *Jeremiah*, *Lamentations*. Chicago: Wilcox & Follett Company, n.d.